READING TO THE CORE

Learning to Read Closely, Critically, and Generatively to Meet Performance Tasks

Elaine Weber ■ Cynthia Schofield ■ Gerri Newnum

Maupin House by
capstone professional

Reading to the Core:
Learning to Read Closely, Critically, and Generatively to Meet Performance Tasks
By Elaine Weber, Cynthia Schofield, and Gerri Newnum

Cover Design: Sarah Bennett
Book Design: Double O Design

Image Credits:
Library of Congress; 63, 77, 81, 95, 96; Mary Tolliver; 69; Shutterstock clipart; cover, 136, 137, 138

Library of Congress Cataloging-in-Publication Data
Weber, Elaine M.
Reading to the core : learning to read closely, critically, and generatively to meet performance tasks / Elaine Weber, Cynthia Schofield, Gerri Newnum.
pages cm
Includes bibliographical references.
ISBN 978-1-62521-522-2 (pb)
1. Guided reading. 2. Reading comprehension. 3. Language arts—Standards—United States. I. Title.
LB1050.377.W44 2013
418'.4071—dc23 2013036511

Maupin House publishes professional resources for K–12 educators. Contact us for tailored, in-school training or to schedule an author for a workshop or conference.
Visit www.maupinhouse.com for free lesson plan downloads.

Maupin House Publishing, Inc. by Capstone Professional
1710 Roe Crest Drive
North Mankato, MN 56003
www.maupinhouse.com
888-262-6135
info@maupinhouse.com

10 9 8 7 6 5 4 3 2 1

Printed in the United States of America in Eau Claire, Wisconsin.
112013 007889

Dedication

To Michael DeVault, Superintendent, and Dr. Judith Pritchett, Chief Academic Officer, who are dedicated to improving the educational opportunities for our students in Macomb County, Michigan.
—*Elaine Weber*

To my daughters, Michael Marie and Courtney Morgan, who judiciously use their voices for justice and equality; carry on the struggle.
—*Cynthia Schofield*

To Jim Newnum, whose patience, inspiration, support, and dedication to education make it all possible.
—*Gerri Newnum*

Acknowledgments

Our sincere thanks to these people:

We especially want to thank Mary Tolliver, who allowed us to share her painting *Out of the Box*. Her art is a powerful voice and beautifully illustrates the power of the visual.

We are particularly grateful to Sue Codere Kelly, whose knowledge, insight, and consistent supply of good humor helped us through several sections of the book.

We thank the Flint Northwestern High School English Department Chair Susan Wolverton and English teachers Kelly Fields and Karen Bailey for their very helpful and practical feedback on several areas of the book.

We want to extend our thanks to the Macomb Intermediate School District (MISD) for providing us with resources and a professional environment in the development, refinement, and implementation of the reading protocol, close and critical reading.

Our sincere thanks to Barbara Reed Nelson, our friend and co-author, who started this journey with us. She has played an instrumental role in the development of this book, and we deeply appreciate her support and her friendship.

TABLE OF CONTENTS

PREFACE

My journey has never been on a straight road. Often, patterns are not recognizable until we are able to view them from a distance. Years ago, my interest and a Google search about critical reading led me to Daniel Kurland's website. His three questions about text initiated a quest for a process that leads students to close and critical reading. His first two questions—**What does the text say?** and **How does the text say it?**—appeared to move the reader effectively to a deeper level of meaning and enabled the reader to answer the last question: **What does the text mean?**

I shared these three questions with committees and colleagues; the questions percolated and were used as the structure for the Michigan Department of Education's (MDE) high school literature units that were developed to meet Michigan's ELA requirements for graduation. In addition, the three questions shaped the reading initiative in Macomb County, Michigan. The goal remained the same: to move students through complex texts—literature and informational—and enable them to ascertain the theme, principal theory, and big ideas in general.

The three questions turned into four questions when Susan Codere Kelly, the standards consultant from MDE, suggested that students needed to connect with the text. So the fourth question was added: **What does the text mean to me?** The intent was that students were encouraged to connect at the big-idea level and not just with a character or smaller detail in the text.

Since then, teachers and students across the county are using the questions to lead to rich conversations in literature circles, deep discussions in Socratic circles, and profound reflective written responses. It is awe-inspiring to witness what students can discover in a piece of text by reading closely and critically.

Standards: 1–3:
What does the text say?

Standards: 4–6:
How does the text say it?

Standards: 7–9:
What does it mean?

In 2009, the Common Core State Standards were being created and I, along with Karen Wixon, represented Michigan as part of the multi-state initiative to shape the standards. In general, the 10 Common Core Reading Anchor Standards ended up reflecting the four questions. In fact, Timothy Shanahan, in one of his addresses to the 2012 International Reading Association Conference, held up the 10 reading anchor standards and said, "The first three standards answer the question 'What does the text say?' And the next three standards answer the question 'How does the text say it?' And the next three standards answer the question 'What does it mean?'"

Through the years, Macomb County and colleagues across Michigan have dedicated themselves to scaffolding students to the pursuit of the literacy needed for the twenty-first century. They have created countless presentations, bookmarks, rubrics, websites, and scaffolding for these four questions. My co-authors and comrades, Cynthia Schofield and Gerri Newnum, have shared vast parts of my journey. They have made numerous presentations on close and critical reading at various state conferences. Our collaborations and conversations have deepened our understanding of close and critical reading. But, we are well aware that knowledge must be shared. All students need to be close and critical readers of complex texts. So, the quest continues.

The creation of the Common Core State Standards supplied fertile ground for this book. Now we have multiple states sharing standards that can be attained through these four simple questions. It is time to share with a broader audience the ways we can use these standards and questions to help students achieve college and career readiness. The journey continues.

Elaine Weber

CHAPTER ONE: **THE POWER TO ENGAGE**

The Power to Engage: A Journey to the Core of Informational Text

Most teachers would agree that the Common Core State Standards (CCSS) have been a game changer for all invested in literacy. The creation of CCSS has enabled states to share a common vision of literacy and has encouraged collaboration among teachers across the United States of America. The timing could not be better. But then perhaps it was not by accident, as the ground was fertile for this endeavor. Everything is aligned. It is the perfect storm: an event arising due to a powerful combined effect of a unique set of circumstances.

Before we discuss our methods of battening down the hatches for that perfect storm, we'd like to assure readers that, first and foremost, we regard ourselves as teachers. Gerri and Cynthia have spent more time teaching than doing anything else. Cynthia still teaches high school English. Gerri became a central office administrator, and Elaine has spent most of her long career as an English language arts consultant at state, county, and district levels. Even when our professional roles have been to assist or guide teachers, we asked them to lend us their students so we could try out strategies. As a result, all three of us know that potholes lurk in the teacher's path. Teaching is not an easy job, despite its many rewards. Some days are even more challenging than others due to the intricacy of some of the work we must do.

Storyteller's View: Why Have We Included the Storyteller's Role?

Today, at the tap of a touch pad, reality provides hefty doses of terror dished out in weighty servings of complex text. How can we cope with the mind-boggling digital memory that slings one text after another before our spinning eyes? Just as important, schools require students to read far more informational text than narration, and the Common Core State Standards reflect that weight. How can teachers help students faced with this monumental text overload to understand it, analyze it, and arrive at some sort of meaning?

This book presents our answer: we can still rely on story as a pathway to understanding informational text. Let's embark on a journey to the core. The chapters ahead present a background of story as a pathway into informational text, for every text has a story behind it or held within it, and awareness of that story often lightens the reader's work.

We too have struggled with informational text, usually wondering what we can do to increase the likelihood of *every* student reaching understanding. We have worked with the Michigan Department of Education's literature units adding informational text, with the Macomb County literature units on close and critical reading, and with excerpts from the Common Core Standards' Appendix B.

Informational Text Inside and Out

Just what makes informational texts so challenging? When a scientist writes for other scientists, the reader can usually slice through complexity with nary a concern, for key vocabulary, essential concepts, and critical events tend to be within the "been there, done that" realm of professional experience known by everyone inside the field. A scientist can, in other words, depend on other scientists to know a number of things and therefore does not need to explain them when writing, just as a mathematician, a chef, a surgeon, and a race car driver can expect a certain amount of basic professional knowledge from colleagues. When we address one of those "insider" texts, the reader's work involves a fair amount of knowledge-seeking to gain the content background essential to the text.

When writing for the general public, however, or even when developing instructional texts for beginners in the discipline, the wise writer turns to the author's craft and oftentimes even the storyteller's strategies to provide a bridge for the reader to cross the confusion gap. A careful reader can draw on an understanding of authors' strategies to help probe to the depths of challenging text and unlock the meaning that lies like a treasure at its core.

Theme: Global Citizenship

Let's begin with an example of a story underlying an informational text—ours. We stumbled upon the theme that ties the texts of this book together for us. Cynthia was driving to Elaine's house for a writing weekend. During her drive, she heard a radio show discussing the 2011 National Assessment of Educational Progress (NAEP) scores. The scores had revealed the alarming decline of twelfth graders' knowledge of the U.S. government and democracy. Furthermore, a 2012 survey by the Montpelier Foundation revealed that only 28 percent of the individuals surveyed

Storyteller's View: The Power of Story

Storytelling has played a meaty role in human existence in a history that weaves its way around almost every documented human event—and probably many never recorded. When people had only oral tradition, stories became a reliable method of relating crucial events without losing key pieces. As we moved on through human history, stories continued to intertwine with facts, at times becoming indistinguishable, as the tale of Orson Welles' *War of the Worlds* radio broadcast and its impact on a terrified American populace revealed. Through the words and sounds in his radio broadcast, Welles created a reality that lived in the minds of his listeners. We'd like to draw on that power.

admitted to reading the entire Constitution of the United States. The facts sent Cynthia on a journey for further data and led to a weekend of rich discussion. Some of the facts uncovered through Google are:

- In the 2010 NAEP, only 23 percent of fourth graders were able to point out the significance of President Washington (first U.S. president, commander in chief of the Continental Army, participant in the Constitutional Convention, or person of significance in the French and Indian War). Twenty-four percent entered inappropriate responses, 45 percent received partial credit, and 7 percent did not respond (Institute of Education Sciences).

- Of the seniors taking the 2010 NAEP, only 12 percent scored "proficient" in history. Seventeen percent grade eight students and 20 percent of grade four students scored "grade-appropriate" levels (Murray 1).

- In a 2011 poll, *Newsweek* found that of 1,000 Americans, 70 percent could not correctly answer the question: "What is the supreme law of the land?" (Dwyer 1).

Reading for an Educated Citizenry

We pondered what an educated citizen would look like in the twenty-first century. We knew it would require not only having the information all citizens should know, but also

- reading closely and learning what a text literally says.
- determining all the mechanisms that authors use to argue a point.
- understanding the power of language to persuade or convince.
- analyzing text critically for bias, marginalizing, and accuracy.
- understanding the text in a larger, critical context.
- responding empathetically to the plight of other human beings.

But what else would be required? We began to ponder what texts would best nurture the identified traits of an educated citizenry. We started to focus on texts that would inform students as well as encourage engaging dialogue. We argued over texts, discovered texts, and finally determined the texts. We expanded our thinking through collaborative dialogue. The result of our conversation and thinking is this book.

Structure of the Book

The following diagram represents the structure of the book.

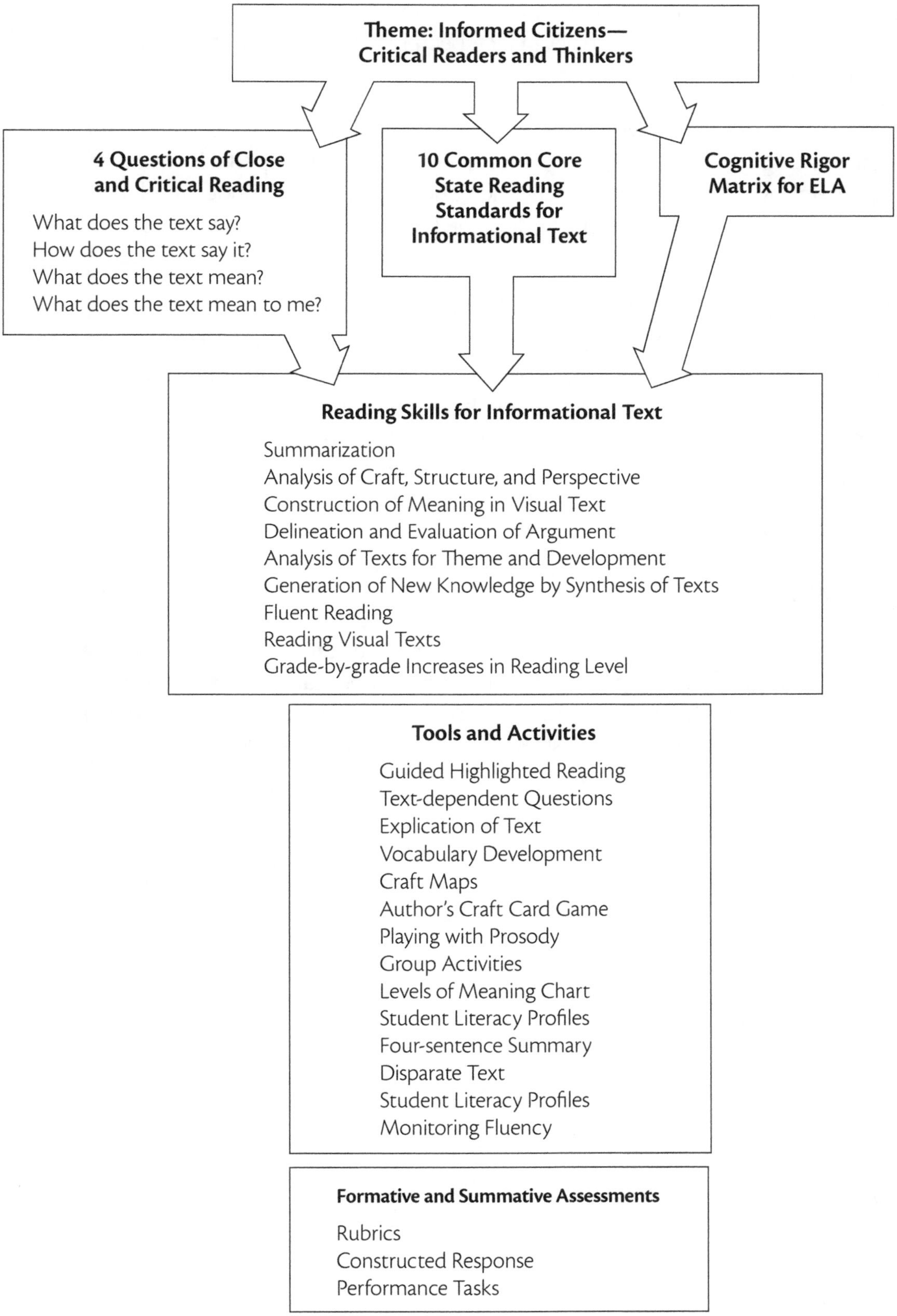

A Winding Road—from What to What?

We have all been charged with reading more informational text. The 2009 NAEP had a text distribution of 50 percent informational in middle school and 70 percent in high school (National Assessment Governing Board 11). We have, in fact, been reading more informational text, yet how can we maximize that process?

For many years, we have worked with teachers and students to develop close and critical reading skills that now align with CCSS. Through four questions, we developed a focus on accessing text first at a literal level; then with inferences and conclusions; then by understanding the craft, structure, and perspectives; and finally by finding the bigger ideas, arguments, theories, and life lessons.

We now know that just gathering knowledge, sorting it, and analyzing it are not enough. We need to do something with it. We added generative reading because we realized that today's students have access to incredible amounts of text. They need to understand how to synthesize those texts to come to new knowledge. We now have the tools to lead students to a point at which they can do that generative thinking with CCSS, the Cognitive Rigor Matrix, and our four questions:

- What does the text say?
- How does the text say it?
- What does the text mean?
- So, what? (What does it mean to me?)

The four questions and their alignment to the Common Core Standards are provided here and in Appendix 1a. Note that additional questions are provided beneath the four questions. The extra questions will not apply to every text, but they will generate thinking and scaffold students to independent close and critical reading skills. They could easily be made into bookmarks for struggling students.

Questions for Close and Critical Reading

CC designations refer to standards from Common Core College and Career Readiness Anchor Standards for Reading.

Question #1—Restatement: What Does the Text Say?	Question #2—Description: How Does the Text Say It?
Write a shortened version of the text containing only the main points and logical inferences. • How would you summarize or write a shortened version of the text containing only the main points? *CC1, CC2* • What is the gist/central idea? *CC1, CC2* •What is the specific textual evidence used to support the central idea? *CC1* • What are the most important ideas/events? *CC1, CC2* • What are the ideas in order of importance or presentation? *CC1* • What ideas might the author be suggesting rather than directly stating? What can you infer (obvious, logical inferences) from these hints or suggestions? *CC1*	**What techniques of craft and structure does the author use in the text? What are the genre, organization, features, word choice, figures of speech, etc.?** • How is the information organized (e.g., time, topic, argument, chapter, scene, stanza, etc.)? *CC5* • What genre does the selection represent? *CC5* • How does the piece open—exposition, lead, etc.? *CC5* • Whose voice did the author choose as narrator? *CC3* • From what point of view was this written? *CC3* • What are the sources of information and fact? Is there more than one source of information? *CC3* • What role does dialogue play in the text? *CC3* • What kind of language is used—dialect, variant spellings, archaic words, etc.? *CC4* • What are the style, mood, and tone? *CC4* • What word choice, imagery, and figures of speech (e.g., simile, metaphor, alliteration, irony, repetition, personification, etc.) does the author use? *CC4* • What diction and sentence structure does the author use, and how do the sections of the text relate to each other—from the sentence and paragraph levels to the section and chapter levels? *CC4*

From *Guided Highlighted Reading* by Weber, Schofield, and Nelson (Maupin House, 2012)

Questions for Close and Critical Reading

CC designations refer to standards from Common Core College and Career Readiness Anchor Standards for Reading.

Question #3—Interpretation: What Does the Text Mean?

What is the theme/thesis of the text and how do the author's choice of content, structure, and craft combine to achieve his/her purpose?

- What is the central idea/thesis/theme of the text? *CC2*
- How does the author support the central idea, thesis, or theme with ideas and details? *CC2*
- What are the purposes, ends, and objectives? *CC2*
- What is the author's stance/perspective toward the topic? *CC6*
- How does the author use language: dialect, variant spellings, archaic words, formal or informal words, etc., to shape the tone (the author's attitude toward the subject) and the meaning of the piece? *CC6*
- How does the author use point of view, style, mood, tone, text features, imagery, figures of speech (e.g., simile, metaphor, alliteration, irony, repetition, onomatopoeia, personification, etc.) and the lead, etc., to achieve his/her purpose (author's intent)? *CC6*
- Why does the author choose the method of presentation? *CC8*
- What are the concepts that make the reasoning possible, what assumptions underlie the concepts, and what implications follow from the concepts? *CC7, CC8*
- What does the author want the reader to believe? *CC7, CC8*
- What is the quality of information collected; Are the sources sufficient, relevant, credible, current? *CC7, CC8*
- Who or what is not represented? Why? *CC7, CC8*

Question #4—Application: So, What?

Evaluation and integration: What does the theme/thesis mean in your life and/or in the lives of others—text-to-self, text-to-text, and/or text-to-world?

Text(s)-to-self: *CC7*

- What does this remind me of in my life?
- What is this similar to in my life?
- How is this different from my life?
- Has something like this ever happened to me?
- How does this relate to my life?
- What were my feelings when I read this?

Text(s)-to-text: *CC9*

- What does this remind me of in another book I've read?
- How is this text similar to other things I've read?
- How is this different from other books I've read?
- Have I read about something like this before?

Text(s)-to-world: *CC7*

- What does this remind me of in the real world?
- How is this text similar to things that happen in the real world?
- How does this differ from things that happen in the real world?
- How did that part relate to the world around me?

From *Guided Highlighted Reading* by Weber, Schofield, and Nelson (Maupin House, 2012)

Before continuing on our journey, it is important to review the College and Career Readiness Anchor Standards for Reading. Though we will refer to them throughout the book, it is helpful to read them in their entirety and observe the interrelationships between them. They have played a crucial role in the rethinking of literacy and in the dialogue and collaboration between states. They have expanded the dialogue, a dialogue which we are entering through this text.

College and Career Readiness Anchor Standards for Reading

Key Ideas and Details
1. Read closely to determine what the text says explicitly and to make logical inferences from it; cite specific textual evidence when writing or speaking to support conclusions drawn from the text.
2. Determine central ideas or themes of a text and analyze their development; summarize the key supporting details and ideas.
3. Analyze how and why individuals, events, and ideas develop and interact over the course of a text.
Craft and Structure
4. Interpret words and phrases as they are used in a text, including determining technical, connotative, and figurative meanings, and analyze how specific word choices shape meaning or tone.
5. Analyze the structure of texts, including how specific sentences, paragraphs, and larger portions of the text (e.g., a section, chapter, scene, or stanza) relate to each other and the whole..
6. Assess how point of view or purpose shapes the content and style of a text.
Integration of Knowledge and Ideas
7. Integrate and evaluate content presented in diverse media and formats, including visually and quantitatively, as well as in words.
8. Delineate and evaluate the argument and specific claims in a text, including the validity of the reasoning as well as the relevance and sufficiency of the evidence.
9. Analyze how two or more texts address similar themes or topics in order to build knowledge or to compare the approaches the authors take.
Range of Reading and Level of Text Complexity
10. Read and comprehend complex literary and informational texts independently and proficiently.

Depth of Knowledge (DOK) and Cognitive Rigor Matrix

The College and Career Readiness Anchor Standards for Reading drive instruction; in addition, they place high expectations upon students. However, it is the Depth of Knowledge (DOK) component that adds another dimension to the standards by expanding the rigor of curriculum and assessments. It impacts instruction and encourages the close, critical, and generative reading students will need in the twenty-first century. Furthermore, it promotes a deeper discourse in the classroom and between teachers.

DOK is particularly effective in helping teachers develop performance tasks. DOK levels reflect the complexity of cognitive processes required by an assessment. Therefore, when developing a performance task, a teacher needs to provide a series of constructed responses at lower DOK levels prior to the performance task at a higher DOK level. The scaffolding of DOK levels provides a teacher and the student with crucial information as to where the student is proficient and scaffolds him or her to the higher-order thinking processes he or she needs to integrate into daily life.

Hess's Cognitive Rigor Matrix

DOK will be discussed throughout the chapters, but closely peruse the chart on the next page, Hess's Cognitive Rigor Matrix & Curricular Examples: Applying Webb's Depth of Knowledge to Bloom's Cognitive Process Dimensions—ELA.

Hess's Cognitive Rigor Matrix & Curricular Examples: Applying Webb's Depth-of-Knowledge to Bloom's Cognitive Process Dimensions—ELA

Revised Bloom's Taxonomy	Webb's DOK Level 1 Recall & Reproduction	Webb's DOK Level 2 Skills & Concepts	Webb's DOK Level 3 Strategic Thinking/Reasoning	Webb's DOK Level 4 Extended Thinking
Remember Retrieve knowledge from long-term memory, recognize, recall, locate, identify	• Recall, recognize, or locate basic facts, details, events, or ideas explicit in texts • Read words orally in connected text with fluency & accuracy			
Understand Construct meaning, clarify, paraphrase, represent, translate, illustrate, give examples, classify, categorize, summarize, generalize, infer a logical conclusion, predict, compare/contrast, match like ideas, explain, construct models	• Identify or describe literary elements (characters, setting, sequence, etc.) • Select appropriate words when intended meaning/ definition is clearly evident • Describe/explain who, what, where, when, or how • Define/describe facts, details, terms, principles • Write simple sentences	• Specify, explain, show relationships; explain why, cause-effect • Give non-examples/examples • Summarize results, concepts, ideas • Make basic inferences or logical predictions from data or texts • Identify main ideas or accurate generalizations of texts • Locate information to support explicit-implicit central ideas	• Explain, generalize, or connect ideas using supporting evidence (quote, example, text reference) • Identify/ make inferences about explicit or implicit themes • Describe how word choice, point of view, or bias may affect the readers' interpretation of a text • Write multi-paragraph composition for specific purpose, focus, voice, tone, & audience	• Explain how concepts or ideas specifically relate to other content domains or concepts • Develop generalizations of the results obtained or strategies used and apply them to new problem situations
Apply Carry out or use a procedure in a given situation; carry out (apply to a familiar task), or use (apply) to an unfamiliar task	• Use language structure (pre/ suffix) or word relationships (synonym/antonym) to determine meaning of words • Apply rules or resources to edit spelling, grammar, punctuation, conventions, word use • Apply basic formats for documenting sources	• Use context to identify the meaning of words/phrases • Obtain and interpret information using text features • Develop a text that may be limited to one paragraph • Apply simple organizational structures (paragraph, sentence types) in writing	• Apply a concept in a new context • Revise final draft for meaning or progression of ideas • Apply internal consistency of text organization and structure to composing a full composition • Apply word choice, point of view, style to impact readers'/ viewers' interpretation of a text	• Illustrate how multiple themes (historical, geographical, social) may be interrelated • Select or devise an approach among many alternatives to research a novel problem

Hess's Cognitive Rigor Matrix & Curricular Examples: Applying Webb's Depth-of-Knowledge to Bloom's Cognitive Process Dimensions—ELA

Revised Bloom's Taxonomy	Webb's DOK Level 1 Recall & Reproduction	Webb's DOK Level 2 Skills & Concepts	Webb's DOK Level 3 Strategic Thinking/Reasoning	Webb's DOK Level 4 Extended Thinking
Analyze Break into constituent parts, determine how parts relate, differentiate between relevant-irrelevant, distinguish, focus, select, organize, outline, find coherence, deconstruct (e.g., for bias or point of view)	• Identify whether specific information is contained in graphic representations (e.g., map, chart, table, graph, T-chart, diagram) or text features (e.g., headings, subheadings, captions) • Decide which text structure is appropriate to audience and purpose	• Categorize, compare literary elements, terms, facts/details, events • Identify use of literary devices • Analyze format, organization & internal text structure (signal words, transitions, semantic clues) of different texts • Distinguish: relevant-irrelevant information; fact/opinion • Identify characteristic text features; distinguish between texts, genres	• Analyze information within data sets or texts • Analyze interrelationships among concepts, issues, problems • Analyze or interpret author's craft (literary devices, viewpoint, or potential bias) to create or critique a text • Use reasoning, planning, and evidence to support inferences	• Analyze multiple sources of evidence, or multiple works by the same author, or across genres, time periods, themes • Analyze complex/abstract themes, perspectives, concepts • Gather, analyze, and organize multiple information sources • Analyze discourse styles
Evaluate Make judgments based on criteria, check, detect inconsistencies or fallacies, judge, critique			• Cite evidence and develop a logical argument for conjectures • Describe, compare, and contrast solution methods • Verify reasonableness of results • Justify or critique conclusions drawn	• Evaluate relevancy accuracy, & completeness of information from multiple sources • Apply understanding in a novel way, provide argument or justification for the application
Create Reorganize elements into new patterns/structures, generate, hypothesize, design, plan, produce	• Brainstorm ideas, concepts, problems, or perspectives related to a topic or concept	• Generate conjectures or hypotheses based on observations or prior knowledge and experience	• Synthesize information within one source or text • Develop a complex model for a given situation • Develop an alternative solution	• Synthesize information across multiple sources or texts • Articulate a new voice, alternate theme, new knowledge or perspective

Guiding Questions for Our Readers

Thinking is never an isolated event. Even when we are alone, we carry the words, thoughts, and questions of others in our internal dialogues. Each of us has been shaped by the people and events of our lives. The majority of our lives has been spent with teachers, so as you begin your journey through this book, we encourage you to consider the following questions. These queries by fellow teachers have served as our guideposts. When we wandered off the trail, they remained visible and led us back to our quest. We realize that some answers have been answered in greater depth and detail than others. However, we have included them because the dialogue must continue and this book is merely an interruption in the conversation.

- How can I use informational text to help my students develop deeper understanding?

- If I am an English teacher,
  - How can I marry informational text with literature to enrich/enhance the reading experience? (How might recent research about the underdeveloped adolescent brain help my students understand *Romeo and Juliet*?)
  - How can I expand the ideas in literature to help develop understanding of informational text? (What can I do with the ideas in *The Outsiders*?)

- If I am a content-area teacher,
  - How can I help my students read literally and critically to determine author's intent and perspective? (How can I help my students recognize the biases that are shaped by the author's perspective? The author's presentation of details and choice of words can privilege some concepts and marginalize others.)
  - How can I help my students understand how to access the specific content <u>and</u> the big ideas in the texts they read? (How might I work with informational texts to help students begin with the life cycle of the caterpillar and move to an understanding of <u>order</u> and <u>organization</u>?)

- What strategies, tools, and activities are available for me to use with complex informational texts?

Chapter One Works Cited

Dwyer, Devin. "United States of Ignorants? Americans Don't Know Constitution, Surveys Find." *ABC News*. 24 March 2011. Web. 17 July 2013.

Hess, Karen K. "Hess's Cognitive Rigor Matrix." National Center for the Improvement of Educational Assessment. 2011. Web. 13 July 2013.

Institute of Education Sciences: National Center for Educational Statistics. "2010 NAEP Questions Tool: U.S. History: National Data." U.S. Government. n.d. Web. 27 August 2013.

Murry, Michael. "Are You Smarter Than a Twelfth Grader?" *ABC News*. 14 June 2011. Web. 17 July 2013.

U.S. Department of Education. "25 American History Facts Most Students Don't Know." *CollegeStats*. n.d. Web. 17 July 2013.

U. S. Government National Assessment Governing Board. *Reading Framework for the 2009 National Assessment of Educational Progress*. Washington, D.C.: Government Printing Office, September 2008. Web. 17 July 2013.

CHAPTER TWO: **CLOSE READING**

Discovering What the Text Is Saying?

Close and Critical Reading in Michigan

Danielle McNamara and her writing partners in an article in the 2007 text *Reading Comprehension Strategies: Theory, Interventions, and Technologies*, note: "It [close reading] involves almost everything, from the smallest linguistic item to the largest issues of literacy understanding and judgment" (McNamara et al. 480).

Over the past decade, many reading initiatives in Michigan have used four basic questions packaged under the heading "Close and Critical Reading" to move students' thinking with text. A reader is to move from a "literal" understanding of the text's message to a critical analysis of how the text was constructed to determine its meaning or big idea and finally to the personalization of the meaning to the individual reader. Around 2006, the newly adopted Michigan high school content expectations for English language arts guided the development of literature units using the four close and critical reading questions to weave together disparate and related texts to determine overarching themes. Since that time, Mission Literacy, the result of a network of Michigan educators' efforts to improve adolescent literacy, has added other work being done in Michigan featuring the four questions to guide students' thinking with complex text. (Do a search for "mission literacy." The site should come up under "Michigan Mission's possible.")

Story Teller's View: Supreme Court Justices

Controversy over how to interpret subtle text is surprisingly common—reaching even Supreme Court justices. As a *New York Times* opinion piece reveals, Justice Antonin Scalia, writing the *majority* opinion, included a famous line about fences from Robert Frost's poem "Mending Wall," giving it an interpretation many believe a close reading of Frost's poem reveals. An exchange between two Supreme Court justices shows just how far-reaching controversy over text can be. To involve students in this, read enough about the controversy between Justices Scalia and Breyer (search directions below) to explain it to students. Then, give students a copy of Frost's "Mending Wall" and a prompt: **What is Robert Frost's most likely belief about walls/fences as revealed in this poem?** Then, provide students with the following *New York Times* articles, each of which defends a *different* interpretation of the poet's position on fences. Ask students if *their* position has changed after reading the articles.

1. Find the *New York Times* article by doing a search on "Justice Scalia's Poetic License."

2. Find the opposing point of view in a letter to the editor by doing a search on "Scalia Wasn't Wrong on Frost."

Developing a Summary

The close and critical reading question in the box on the next page and the first three CCSS reading anchor standards are aligned and require students to identify what the text is actually saying explicitly and implicitly, with the conclusions, big idea, and development of the ideas put into a summary. However, direction from the Common Core Reading Anchor standards gives a new texture to "reading close." They direct us to read, determine, analyze, and support with evidence. The Partnership for Assessment of Readiness College and Careers (PARCC), a twenty-two-state consortium working together to develop next-generation K–12 assessments in English and math, describes close, analytic reading as "...thoroughly and methodically, encouraging students to read and reread deliberately..." (PARCC Section 3). They further claim that students will be empowered to better understand the elements of the text: central ideas, supporting details, sentences, individual words, and development of ideas in the text.

What does the text say?

CCSS Key Ideas and Details

1. Read closely to determine what the text says explicitly and to make logical inferences from it; cite specific textual evidence when writing or speaking to support conclusions drawn from the text.
2. Determine central ideas or themes of a text and analyze their development; summarize the key supporting details and ideas.
3. Analyze how and why individuals, events, and ideas develop and interact over the course of a text.

Text Selection: Framing the Reading

We have tried to find text that fits our theme of world citizenship as well as text that has the potential to offer multiple perspectives or change a perspective. Our initial dialogue regarding an educated citizenry brought up the fact that we as Americans are citizens in a global world. Citizenship in the broadest sense is our relationship to one another—no matter what race, creed, color, religion, or country of origin. It seems to be a good message any time to remind one another that we are our brother's keeper. Carl Sagan reminds us that we are all on this earth together and, to date, we have nowhere else to go.

The following excerpt from a speech by William Jennings Bryan, Imperialism, delivered August 8, 1900, was selected as the first text in this book because it expresses the confidence Bryan had in the ability of an enlightened citizenry to govern itself. A central tenet of this book is to contribute to the discussion of what an enlightened and literate citizenry looks like in the twenty-first century.

> "The Republicans say that this nation is in the hands of destiny; Washington believed that not only the destiny of our own nation but the destiny of the republican form of government throughout the world was entrusted to American hands. Immeasurable responsibility! The destiny of this Republic is in the hands of its own people, and upon the success of the experiment here rests the hope of humanity. No exterior force can disturb this Republic, and no foreign influence should be permitted to change its course. What the future has in store for this nation no one has authority to declare, but each individual has his own idea of the nation's mission, and he owes it to his country as well as to himself to contribute as best he may to the fulfillment of that mission. . . .
>
> I can conceive of a national destiny surpassing the glories of the present and the past—a destiny which meets the responsibilities of today and measures up to the possibilities of the future. Behold a republic, resting securely upon the foundation stones quarried by revolutionary patriots from the mountain of eternal truth—a republic applying in practice and proclaiming to the world the self-evident propositions that all men are created equal; that they are endowed with inalienable rights; that governments are instituted among men to secure these rights, and that governments derive their just powers from the consent of the governed. Behold a republic in which civil and religious liberty stimulate all to earnest endeavor and in which the law restrains every hand uplifted for a neighbor's injury—a republic in which every citizen is a sovereign, but in which no one cares to wear a crown. Behold a republic standing erect while empires all around are bowed beneath the weight of their own armaments—a republic whose flag is loved while other flags are only feared. Behold a republic increasing in population, in wealth, in strength and in influence, solving the problems of civilization and hastening the coming of an universal brotherhood—a republic which shakes thrones and dissolves aristocracies by its silent example and gives light and inspiration to those who sit in darkness. Behold a republic gradually but surely becoming the supreme moral factor in the world's progress and the accepted arbiter of the world's disputes—a republic whose history, like the path of the just, 'is as the shining light that shineth more and more unto the perfect day.'"

Levels of Support for Close Reading

The first three Common Core Standards, known as the "evidence" standards, have within them the guidance to read text closely enough to know what the text says, gather support for the ideas in the text with evidence, and provide enough information to write a summary. The following demonstrates how this process works with the passage above.

1. **What does the text say explicitly? (CCSSR1)** *In this excerpt, Bryan conceives of a destiny for the republic that goes beyond meeting the responsibilities of today, the past, and the possibilities of the future. He claims that the future of the republic form of government is in the hands of the people, and is the hope for humanity because it is built on rights given in the Declaration of Independence and it has a government run by its citizens. The republic stands erect, whereas others yield to armament. It is a model, an arbitrator, and an inspiration to others. It is flourishing because it is self-governing and not ruled by another state.*

2. **What is the logical inference from this perspective? (CCSSR1)** *The American republic has met its responsibilities because it is self-governing, it is based on the principles of the Declaration of Independence, and it is not ruled by another state.*

3. **What is the conclusion that can be drawn from this text? (CCSSR1)** *Self-governing republics have a positive destiny.*

4. **What is the textual evidence? (CCSSR1)** *The author (William Jennings Bryan) perceives the destiny of the American republic to be a self-governing one.*
   - *The nation's strength has its base in the work of the patriots who fought in the American Revolution.*
   - *Americans have inalienable rights.*
   - *The American flag is loved, not feared.*
   - *Bryan believes America is hastening the arrival of a "universal brotherhood."*

5. **What is the central idea or theme? (CCSSR2)** *Self-governance is the foundation of a successful republic.*

6. **What are the supporting details and ideas? (CCSSR2)** *Success of the American republic is based on*
   - *Individual concepts of a mission for the nation.*
   - *Principles set forth in the Declaration of Independence.*
   - *The fact that government is instituted among its people.*
   - *Provisions for civil and religious freedom.*
   - *Sovereignty of every citizen.*

7. **How did ideas develop and interact over the course of this text? (CCSSR3)** *This text follows a cause-and-effect and description format. The effect of America's republic is that it is sustained, a model, an arbitrator, and an inspiration to others. The second paragraph provides the attributes of the republic of America.*

There are many ways to teach students how to write a summary, but a summary that meets CCSS would have a rubric such as the one following, which is also in Appendix 2a as a reproducible item:

Summary Rubric

CC Reading Anchor Standards	3 Complete	2 Partial	1 Minimal	Score
1. Read closely to determine what the text says explicitly and to make logical inferences from it; cite specific textual evidence when writing or speaking to support conclusions drawn from the text.	Reading Anchor # 1 Response: • states what the text says explicitly. (3 points) • makes logical inferences and cites specific textual evidence to support conclusions drawn from the text. (3 points)	Reading Anchor #1 Response: • includes much of what the text says explicitly. (2 points) • makes some logical inferences and cites general textual evidence to support some of the conclusions drawn from the text. (2 points)	Reading Anchor #1 Response: • includes little of what the text says explicitly. (1 point) • makes few logical inferences and gives little support drawn from the text. (1 point)	**__/6 pts.**
2. Determine central ideas or themes of a text and analyze their development; summarize the key supporting details and ideas.	Reading Anchor #2 Response: • summarizes using clearly identified central or main ideas. (3 points) • supports central ideas well with key details and ideas from the text. (3 points)	Reading Anchor #2 Response: • summarizes using partially or ineffectively identified central or main ideas. (2 points) • supports central ideas with some details and ideas from the text. (2 points)	Reading Anchor #2 Response: • summarizes using inaccurately identified central or main ideas. (1 point) • supports central ideas with few details and ideas from the text. (1 point)	**__/6 pts.**
3. Analyze how and why individuals, events, and ideas develop and interact over the course of a text.	Reading Anchor #3 Response expertly analyzes in detail where, when, why, and how events, ideas, and characters develop and interact. (Literature) (3 points)	Reading Anchor #3 Response partially analyzes in detail where, when, why, and how events, ideas, and characters develop and interact. (Literature) (2 points)	Reading Anchor #3 Response analyzes with little detail where, when, why, and how events, ideas, and characters develop and interact. (Literature) (1 point)	**__/3pts.** **Total** **__/15pts.**

From *Guided Highlighted Reading* by Weber, Schofield, and Nelson (Maupin House, 2012)

Sample Summary

The author provides his perspective on the destiny of America's republic as an experiment in the hands of its own people; on the success of which rests the hope for humanity. He predicts the national destiny is to continue to be successful and meet the possibilities of the future. We are told to behold a republic practicing the rights derived from the "mountain of eternal truth." The republic, he argues, is a model nation respected by others, that is increasing, "...in population, in wealth, in strength and in influence." According to the author, the republic was becoming a supreme moral factor and an arbiter for disputes. It is "the shining light that shineth more and more unto the perfect day," because it is "self-governing and not ruled by another state."

Hess's Cognitive Rigor Matrix—"Understand" Segment. When students write a summary or summarize a text, they are functioning at the following level indicated below on Karen Hess's Cognitive Rigor Matrix.

Revised Bloom's Taxonomy	**Webb's DOK Level 1 Recall & Reproduction**	**Webb's DOK Level 2 Basic Skills & Concepts**	**Webb's DOK Level 3 Strategic Thinking/ Reasoning**	**Webb's DOK Level 4 Extended Thinking**
Understand	• Identify or describe literary elements (characters, setting, sequence, etc.) • Select appropriate words when intended meaning/ definition is clearly evident • Describe/explain who, what, where, when, or how • Define/describe facts, details, terms, principles • Write simple sentences	• Specify, explain, show relationships; explain why, cause-effect • Give non-examples/ examples • Summarize results, concepts, ideas • Make basic inferences or logical predictions from data or texts • Identify main ideas or accurate generalizations of texts • Locate information to support explicit-implicit central ideas	• Explain, generalize, or connect ideas using supporting evidence (quote, example, text reference) • Identify/ make inferences about explicit or implicit themes • Describe how word choice, point of view, or bias may affect the readers' interpretation of a text • Write multi-paragraph composition for specific purpose, focus, voice, tone, & audience	• Explain how concepts or ideas specifically relate to *other* content domains or concepts • Develop generalizations of the results obtained or strategies used and apply them to new problem situations

Summaries are the evidence that the student knows what the text says. Summarizing, accompanied by note-taking, is one of the "big" nine instructional strategies that Marzano, Pickering, and Pollock found to improve student achievement. Their research effect size for the summary and note-taking combination (the impact of using summary and note-taking in the classroom) was the second largest, second only to the effect size for identifying similarities and differences (Marzano et al. 7). Other research suggests that instruction and practice in summarizing will improve not only students' ability to summarize text, but also their overall comprehension of text content (Farstrup). Not only does summarizing text have a powerful effect, but it is one of the most common ways people are asked to think about text throughout their schooling and careers.

Text-dependent Questions

With the Common Core State Reading Standards, students are guided to do close reading by responding to questions that are called "text-dependent questions." This kind of question plunges students deep into the text, asking them to analyze, synthesize, and evaluate what they might find within the text. This activity places increased focus on the text itself. Text-dependent questions are designed to bring insight to the reader from the text that was not recognized in previous readings.

Teacher Preparation for Text-dependent Questions

ACHIEVE (an organization of bipartisan governors and corporate leaders dedicated to supporting standards-based education reform efforts across the states) has provided a set of guidelines for the preparation of the text. The guidelines provided by ACHIEVE in "A Guide to Creating Text-Dependent Questions for Close Analytic Reading" suggest that the teacher consider several points in preparation for creating the text-dependent questions:

- Analyze paragraphs on a sentence-by-sentence basis and sentences on a word-by-word basis to determine the role played by individual paragraphs, sentences, phrases, or words.
- Investigate how meaning can be altered by changing key words and why an author may have chosen one word over another.
- Probe each argument in persuasive text, each idea in informational text, and each key detail in literary text, and observe how these build to a whole.
- Examine how shifts in the direction of an argument or explanation are achieved and the impact of those shifts.
- Question why authors choose to begin and end when they do.
- Note and assess patterns of writing and what they achieve.
- Consider what the text leaves uncertain or unstated. (Student Achievement Partners 1)

Revisiting the Text: Text-dependent Questions

Let's take another look at Bryan's speech.

> "The Republicans say that this nation is in the hands of destiny; Washington believed that not only the destiny of our own nation but the destiny of the republican form of government throughout the world was entrusted to American hands. Immeasurable responsibility! The destiny of this Republic is in the hands of its own people, and upon the success of the experiment here rests the hope of humanity. No exterior force can disturb this Republic, and no foreign influence should be permitted to change its course. What the future has in store for this nation no one has authority to declare, but each individual has his own idea of the nation's mission, and he owes it to his country as well as to himself to contribute as best he may to the fulfillment of that mission. . . . *continued —*

> I can conceive of a national destiny surpassing the glories of the present and the past—a destiny which meets the responsibilities of today and measures up to the possibilities of the future. Behold a republic, resting securely upon the foundation stones quarried by revolutionary patriots from the mountain of eternal truth—a republic applying in practice and proclaiming to the world the self-evident propositions that all men are created equal; that they are endowed with inalienable rights; that governments are instituted among men to secure these rights, and that governments derive their just powers from the consent of the governed. Behold a republic in which civil and religious liberty stimulate all to earnest endeavor and in which the law restrains every hand uplifted for a neighbor's injury—a republic in which every citizen is a sovereign, but in which no one cares to wear a crown. Behold a republic standing erect while empires all around are bowed beneath the weight of their own armaments—a republic whose flag is loved while other flags are only feared. Behold a republic increasing in population, in wealth, in strength and in influence, solving the problems of civilization and hastening the coming of an universal brotherhood—a republic which shakes thrones and dissolves aristocracies by its silent example and gives light and inspiration to those who sit in darkness. Behold a republic gradually but surely becoming the supreme moral factor in the world's progress and the accepted arbiter of the world's disputes—a republic whose history, like the path of the just, 'is as the shining light that shineth more and more unto the perfect day.'"

The following text-dependent questions address CCSS 1, 2, and 3.

General Understanding of the Text

In this excerpt, the author organizes the discussion around the "destiny" of the republic. Trace the argument giving evidence from the text.

The author argues that America was entrusted with this republic and the stakes were high: "success of the experiment here rests the hope for humanity." He claims that the future of the republic resides in the mission of every individual. The republic has demonstrated success for the past and the present and will meet the possibilities of the future. Evidence for this prediction comes from the foundation upon which it was built: rights and principles from the "foundation stones quarried by revolutionary patriots." He claims that the republic is a model, an example, an arbiter, a moral factor, and is respected among world nations. It is "increasing in population, in wealth, in strength, and in influence." The fact that the republic is self-governing and not ruled by any other state accounts for its success.

Key Supporting Details

According to this excerpt, what does "self-governing" entail for the individual citizen?

The author states that "...each individual has his own idea of the nation's mission, and he owes it to his country as well as to himself to contribute as best he may to the fulfillment of that mission. . . ." Further he claims that "every citizen is a sovereign but in which no one cares to wear a crown."

Author's Purpose

Why did the author write this speech? Give evidence for your response.

The author was responding to the Republicans' claim regarding the destiny of the republic. The author makes the point that the republic is successful from the past to the present and into the future because it is self-governing, fueled by the individual's ideas for the mission of the nation, and built on the "foundation stones quarried by revolutionary patriots."

Vocabulary

The word *destiny* means either "preordained future" or "realizable purpose of life" or "something that predetermines events." Select a definition that best fits Bryan's argument and support it with evidence from the text.

The author states that the republic is "resting securely upon the foundation stones quarried by revolutionary patriots from the mountain of eternal truth." This, he suggests, is the force or agency that predetermined the success of the republic, "... applying in practice and proclaiming to the world the self-evident propositions...." The definition involving predetermination is the closest, although "preordained future" comes close as well.

Inferences

When the republic is described, the author reveals what he doesn't value in governments. Identify what is cast negatively. Provide evidence from the text.

The author claims that in the republic "every citizen is a sovereign, but in which no one cares to wear a crown." In other words, citizens have collective power but not the sole power.

He states the republic "...shakes thrones and dissolves aristocracies by its silent example and gives light and inspiration to those who sit in darkness." Silence is at times more powerful for the unfortunate or unenlightened than more powerful action.

He contrasts the republic to the empires who are bowed by the weight of their own armament, suggesting that the cost of warfare is heavy to bear.

CCSS by Grade Level

CCSS Anchor standards represent the kind of skills and knowledge students need at the end of their K–12 schooling to enter the college or career phase of their lives. The road to the anchor standards is outlined standard by standard and grade by grade. The intent of the standards is to grow reading skills grade by grade with the Common Core Reading for Information standards from kindergarten to college and career readiness.

Grade-level CCSSRI 1, 2, and 3 from fourth grade to twelfth grade. As the standards progress up the grade levels, the language in the standard that indicates new expectations is boldfaced.

Standard 1

Grade 4. Refer to details and examples in a text when explaining what the text says explicitly and when drawing inferences from the text.

Grade 5. Quote accurately from a text when explaining what the text says explicitly and when drawing inferences from the text.

Grade 6. Cite textual evidence to support analysis of what the text says explicitly as well as inferences drawn from the text.

Grade 7. Cite **several pieces** of textual evidence to support analysis of what the text says explicitly as well as inferences drawn from the text.

Grade 8. Cite the textual evidence that **most strongly** supports an analysis of what the text says explicitly as well as inferences drawn from the text.

Grades 9–10. Cite **strong and thorough** textual evidence to support analysis of what the text says explicitly as well as inferences drawn from the text.

Grades 11–12. Cite strong and thorough textual evidence to support analysis of what the text says explicitly as well as inferences drawn from the text, **including determining where the text leaves matters uncertain.**

Standard 2

Grade 4. Determine the main idea of a text and explain how it is supported by key details; summarize the text.

Grade 5. Determine **two or more** main ideas of a text and explain how they are supported by key details; summarize the text.

Grade 6. Determine **a central idea** of a text and **how it is conveyed through particular details;** provide a summary of the text distinct from personal opinions or judgments.

Grade 7. Determine **two or more** central ideas in a text **and analyze their development over the course of the text;** provide an **objective** summary of the text.

Grade 8. Determine a central idea of a text and analyze its development over the course of the text, including its **relationship to supporting ideas;** provide an objective summary of the text.

Grades 9–10. Determine a central idea of a text and analyze its development over the course of the text, including **how it emerges and is shaped and refined by specific details;** provide an objective summary of the text.

Grades 11–12. Determine **two or more** central ideas of a text and analyze their development over the course of the text, **including how they interact and build on one another to provide a complex analysis;** provide an objective summary of the text.

Standard 3

Grade 4. Explain events, procedures, ideas, or concepts in a historical, scientific, or technical text, including what happened and why, based on specific information in the text.

Grade 5. Explain the **relationships or interactions between two or more individuals, events, ideas, or concepts** in a historical, scientific, or technical text based on specific information in the text.

Grade 6. Analyze in detail how a key individual, event, or idea is introduced, illustrated, and elaborated in a text (e.g., through examples or anecdotes).

Grade 7. Analyze the **interactions between** individuals, events, and ideas in a text (e.g., **how ideas influence individuals or events, or how individuals influence ideas or events**).

Grade 8. Analyze how a text **makes connections among and distinctions between** individuals, ideas, or events (e.g., **through comparisons, analogies, or categories**).

Grades 9–10. Analyze how the author **unfolds an analysis or series of ideas or events, including the order in which the points are made, how they are introduced and developed,** and the connections that are drawn between them.

Grades 11–12. Analyze a complex **set of ideas or sequence of events and explain how specific individuals, ideas, or events interact and develop over the course of the text.**

Scaffolding Students Who Need Support

Vocabulary and Reading Development

Being able to read and understand text relies upon knowledge of vocabulary. For the adolescent reader, knowledge of vocabulary, according to the U.S. Government Institute of Education Sciences' (IES) August 2008 publication *Improving Adolescent Literacy: Effective Classroom and Intervention Practices*, was the number-one recommendation for improving the reading of adolescents. The study calls for direct, explicit instruction in all content-area classes.

Storyteller's View: Close Reading of the Pledge of Allegiance

Teaching students to read closely carries a load of concern no matter how many class periods we devote to it, yet a much-beloved comedian offered a perfect example many years ago. Red Skelton carefully laid out the meaning of the entire Pledge of Allegiance, one key bit at a time, just the way we need to address any complex text.

In 1969, Red Skelton presented an explication of the Pledge of Allegiance that has continued to wrench American hearts all these years. The entire text is available on the Red Skelton webpage in video, audio, and print formats. We highly recommend it.

The sample we have chosen comes from the conclusion, where we will do something similar to what Skelton does, though not with the poignancy of his presentation:

With Liberty *(The state of being free in a culture that permits its people to establish their own way of life.)*

And justice *(Fair treatment.)*

For all. *(There are no exclusions. Everyone receives the same treatment.)*

Activity: Explication of Quotations

Red Skelton made the Pledge of Allegiance come alive. Well, students can do the same with quotations—or actually any text. For this activity, provide students with a list of quotations that are appropriate for what they are studying. Working in groups or pairs, students choose one quotation to analyze in detail. They collaborate on the words they will use in the explication. Each student writes his or her own explication. They share with the whole class, or one group or pair shares with another group or pair. Choose one or two to be shared with the entire class.

Note the following quotation:
"… the minority possess their equal rights, which equal law must protect, and to violate would be oppression." –*Thomas Jefferson, Inaugural Address*

…and the explication:
The smaller groups in our society have the same civil liberties, which a balanced legal system should safeguard, and to disregard this would be unjust treatment.

Two Quotations for Explication
"This nation was founded by many men of many nations and backgrounds. It was founded on the principle that all men are created equal, and that the rights of every man are diminished when the rights of one man are threatened." –*John F. Kennedy*

"Educate and inform the whole mass of the people… They are the only sure reliance for the preservation of our liberty." –*Thomas Jefferson*

Activity: Guided Highlighted Reading for Vocabulary

The following activity, Guided Highlighted Reading (GHR) for Vocabulary, supports vocabulary development while keeping the vocabulary in the context of connected text. To prepare the text for GHR, the teacher reads the text to determine the words that would be unknown by the students and that would interfere with comprehension of the text. The teacher writes prompts for the words by supplying the general location of the word and either a definition, a synonym, or an antonym. This activity keeps the vocabulary word in the context of the text.

Directions: Students have a copy of the text and a highlighter pen. The teacher reads the prompts, and the student finds and highlights the word. The strategy is to familiarize students with the potentially unfamiliar vocabulary that may be an impediment to comprehension. Prompts are developed that either provide students with a definition, a synonym, or an antonym. The location of the words is given along with the prompt. For some texts, every line is identified with a number, and for other texts, the paragraphs are numbered. Students highlight the word that is being defined.

Text for Guided Highlighted Reading Practice

1 The Republicans say that this nation is in the hands of destiny; Washington believed that not only the destiny of our own nation but the destiny of the republican form of government throughout the world was entrusted to American hands. Immeasurable responsibility! The destiny of this Republic is in the hands of its own people, and upon the success of the experiment here rests the hope of humanity. No exterior force can disturb this Republic, and no foreign influence should be permitted to change its course. What the future has in store for this nation no one has authority to declare, but each individual has his own idea of the nation's mission, and he owes it to his country as well as to himself to contribute as best he may to the fulfillment of that mission. . . .

2 I can conceive of a national destiny surpassing the glories of the present and the past—a destiny which meets the responsibilities of today and measures up to the possibilities of the future. Behold a republic, resting securely upon the foundation stones quarried by revolutionary patriots from the mountain of eternal truth—a republic applying in practice and proclaiming to the world the self-evident propositions that all men are created equal; that they are endowed with inalienable rights; that governments are instituted among men to secure these rights, and that governments derive their just powers from the consent of the governed. Behold a republic in which civil and religious liberty stimulate all to earnest endeavor and in which the law restrains every hand uplifted for a neighbor's injury—a republic in which every citizen is a sovereign, but in which no one cares to wear a crown. Behold a republic standing erect while empires all around are bowed beneath the weight of their own armaments—a republic whose flag is loved while other flags are only feared. Behold a republic increasing in population, in wealth, in strength and in influence, solving the problems of civilization and hastening the coming of an universal brotherhood—a republic which shakes thrones and dissolves aristocracies by its silent example and gives light and inspiration to those who sit in darkness. Behold a republic gradually but surely becoming the supreme moral factor in the world's progress and the accepted arbiter of the world's disputes—a republic whose history, like the path of the just, "is as the shining light that 'shineth more and more unto the perfect day.'"

The teacher reads the prompts, and the student finds the correct response in the text and highlights it.

1. In paragraph 1, find and highlight the word that means "predetermined." (*destiny*)
2. In paragraph 1, find and highlight the word that means "a form of government in which power is explicitly vested in the people." (*republic*)
3. In paragraph 2, find and highlight the word that means "dug building stone, slate, or the like." (*quarried*)
4. In paragraph 2, find and highlight the word that means "not transferable to another." (*inalienable*)

5. In paragraph 2, find and highlight the word that means "arouse." (*stimulate*)
6. In paragraph 2, find and highlight the word that means "a person or agency whose judgment or opinion is considered authoritative." (*arbiter*)

Activity: Guided Highlighted Reading for Summary

The same strategy can be used for scaffolding students to find the salient points of a text to be able to build a summary. Using the same copy of the text and a different color highlighter, the students can respond to prompts that guide them to the salient points of the text to prepare them for creating a summary.

The teacher reads the prompts, and the students highlight the response.

1. In paragraph #1, find and highlight who claimed our nation was in the hands of destiny. (*Republicans*)
2. In paragraph #1, find and highlight what was labeled the "immeasurable responsibility." ("*the destiny of the republican form of government*")
3. In paragraph #1, find and highlight who the author claims is responsible for the future of the nation. ("*...each individual has his own idea of the nation's mission....*")
4. In paragraph #2, find and highlight what the author thinks about the national destiny. ("*...meets the responsibility of today and measures up to the possibilities of the future.*")
5. In paragraph #2, find and highlight the reference to the Declaration of Independence. (Inference) ("*foundation stones quarried by revolutionary patriots from the mountain of eternal truth*")
6. In paragraph #2, find and highlight who is sovereign, meaning self-governing, and not ruled by any other state. ("*every citizen*")
7. In paragraph #2, find and highlight what the author claims the nation is increasing. ("*in population, in wealth, in strength and in influence*")
8. In paragraph #2, find and highlight what the author says the republic is gradually, but surely becoming. ("*supreme moral factor and accepted arbiter*")
9. In paragraph #2, find and highlight what describes the "path of the just." ("*. . . is as the shining light that shineth more and more unto the perfect day.*")

Activity: Diminishing the Support of GHR

When students are able to respond to your prompting with few or no errors, you can modify the activity by giving students the number of items to be highlighted. You might say, "There are three important points in paragraph 1. Find and highlight them." The next level would be to tell students how many important points are in the whole text. Finally, the students determine the important points on their own or with a partner. If you are moving students up through texts that represent higher Lexile or complexity levels, then continue with GHR. It is important that students see that they are progressing in their reading ability, either through being able to answer comprehension questions or write summaries. You can also raise their reading level by steadily moving them up through texts that increase in reading or Lexile levels.

Documentation of Student Progress

Student Progress on CCR Question 1: What Does the Text Say?

CC Reading Anchor Standards	Fall Rubric Score	Winter Rubric Score	Spring Rubric Score
1. Read closely to determine what the text says explicitly and to make logical inferences from it; cite specific textual evidence when writing or speaking to support conclusions drawn from the text			
2. Determine central ideas or themes of a text and analyze their development; summarize the key supporting details and ideas			
3. Analyze how and why individuals, events, and ideas develop and interact over the course of a text			

Teacher Effectiveness for Close and Critical Reading Question 1: What Does the Text Say?

Students	Fall	Winter	Spring
	Total Rubric Score ______	Total Rubric Score ______	Total Rubric Score ______
	Total Rubric Score ______	Total Rubric Score ______	Total Rubric Score ______
	Total Rubric Score ______	Total Rubric Score ______	Total Rubric Score ______

SIDENOTE—Elaine: Answering the first close and critical reading question, "What does the text say?" once was simply a matter of responding with the literal message, low-level inferences, and a conclusion. CCSS have asked students to dig deeply into the text for a more critical analysis of the message with text-dependent questions and to respond with a summary that is backed up with evidence from the text. It has become close and critical reading on steroids.

Chapter Two Works Cited

Bryan, William Jennings. "Imperialism, 8 August 1990." *Voices of Democracy: U.S. Oratory Project.* National Endowment for the Humanities Project, 2009. Web. 2 October 2013.

Farstrup, A. E., and S. J. Samuels. *What Research Has to Say About Reading Instruction.* Newark, DE: International Reading Association, 2002.

Greenhouse, Linda. "Justice Rules That Congress Overstepped Bounds." 19 April, 1995. Collections: Supreme Court. *The New York Times.* 2 July 2013.

Jefferson, Thomas. "Thomas Jefferson" Quotable Quote. n.d. Web. 15 July 2013.

Kennedy, John F. "John Fitzgerald Kennedy Quotes. *Thinkexist.com.* n.d. Web. 15 July 2013.

Marzano, Robert, Debra J. Pickering, and Jane E. Pollock. *Classroom Instruction That Works: Research-based Strategies for Increasing Student Achievement.* Alexandria, VA: Association for Supervision and Curriculum Development, 2001. Print.

McNamara, Danielle S. *Reading Comprehension Strategies: Theory, Interventions, and Technologies.* Mahwah, NJ: Erlbaum, 2007.

Partnership for Assessment of Readiness for College and Careers. "Structure of the Model Content Frameworks for ELA/Literacy." n.d. Web. 15 July 2013.

Skelton, Red. "Red Skelton's Pledge of Allegiance." Red Skelton. 2009. Web. 8 May 2013.

Student Achievement Partners (ACHIEVE). "A Guide to Creating Text Dependent Questions for Close Analytic Reading." *Steal These Tools: ELA/Literacy.* n.d. Web. 16 July 2013.

U.S. Government Institute of Education Sciences (IES). *Improving Adolescent Literacy: Effective Classroom and Intervention Practices.* What Works Clearinghouse. August 2008. Web. 15 July 2013.

CHAPTER THREE: **AUTHOR'S CRAFT**

Complex Text and Motivation

Just what motivates us to read a complex informational text? If we have sought out the text, most likely we simply want to know more about the subject. If that desire is strong enough, we'll put up with a good deal of trouble in processing the text—even if we are struggling to understand its complexity. On the other hand, what if our interest in the topic is only moderate or even nonexistent? We (and our students) are likely to put far more energy into waging the battle for understanding challenging text if we know more about the author's craft.

Courage and Conviction

English teachers have focused on craft in literature for years, and their students can generally unlock the author's techniques in a story, a poem, or a play. However, those same successful students, given a piece of informational text, are at a loss as to *how* the author manipulates the reader through craft. They often are simply unaware of the power of even such basic tools as word choice, sentence length and complexity, repetition, and parallel structure. Also, many of the same strategies that we appreciate in literature appear in informational text, and rhetorical strategies deepen the possibilities. Showing students how to identify, analyze, and evaluate author's craft strategies helps them to unlock meaning.

Storyteller's View: Author's Craft

At times, skillful authors take on some of the burden for their readers. For example, Robert Sapolsky, writing on the physiological impact of stress in *Why Zebras Don't Get Ulcers*, opens his book with "It's two o'clock in the morning and you're lying in bed." Immediately his reader knows (if the title weren't already a clue) that the book is not going to be a dry, dusty scientific work, even though Sapolsky's content comes to the reader straight from his neuroscience research.

Sapolsky's talent for writing engaging leads sits at the top of a mountain of strategies at the disposal of a skillful author. A careful reader can unlock significantly more meaning by exploring the ways those strategies work in a complex text.

We often work with texts that may appear in multiple versions written by different authors—as in *Romeo and Juliet*, various news stories about the same event, or the definitive biography among many others. The question is not "What happened?" but instead becomes "What makes this version better than all the others? Why did *this* one win a Pulitzer Prize?" The answer generally lies in author's craft, his or her perspective, and the structure.

Those exemplary texts are likely to be more complex—and the reader needs to understand that complexity.

Why?

SIDENOTE—Elaine: Several years ago, 1,500 high school seniors from a fairly high-functioning high school in Macomb County were being taught how to use the four questions of Close and Critical Reading about a text they were reading. When they got to the question "How does the text say it?," they did not really know what we wanted them to write. Even though they were very bright, accomplished students, many were responding by saying, *"in words, sentences and paragraphs...,"* or they reiterated the answer to the first question and put down the summary again. One student wrote his ACT score next to the question to let us know he wasn't stupid ... just clueless.

Just as with literature, informational texts many times retell the same story—multiple news articles covering a cataclysmic event, numerous biographies of one person, two or three scientific articles covering the same discovery. What makes one of the many stand out to win a Pulitzer Prize, make *The New York Times* Best Sellers list for biographies, or be chosen for publication in a premier science journal? Generally, the basic facts remain the same throughout the retellings.

It's not always the facts in the news article—it's often *how* the author writes it that wins the accolades. The losers tend to have a clear rendition of the topic, and meaning is generally fairly accessible. What draws us to the deeper, more subtle complex texts? How can we capture that understanding as readers? Learning to recognize the various components of the author's craft provides the reader with the tools to delve into that complexity for the meaning that lies at its core.

Deeply meaningful texts tend to have a pleasing rhythm to them and draw from the writer's palette of tools in much the same way that an artist selects colors. The results engage the reader and reward deeper analysis with nuggets of meaning that please even the most reluctant reader. A proficient reader can read the complex text, and that is what we are striving for as educators. Otherwise, students are doomed to an understanding of only the simplest level of a complex text. Not only are they deprived of concepts that come with complexity, but they also will never experience the power of the "aha! moments" that occur only with a complex text.

On the other hand, an author may choose a clean, straight path to the meaning she wishes to present. The reader seldom has any trouble understanding, yet the text tends not to be especially interesting, for it presents just the facts. Another approach might appear too mechanical and seem somewhat jerky or even flowery, with unpleasant qualities that tend to annoy rather than engage the reader. Other authors may brush broadly over the top of the content, presenting overarching generalizations that have meaning yet may fall short of any real depth.

Variations in Texts: Gettysburg Address

Do we need to approach each of these versions differently, or will the same reading strategies work for all?

Original Version

What do we need to know and do as readers to understand this text and its complexity?

Four score and seven years ago our fathers brought forth on this continent, a new nation, conceived in Liberty, and dedicated to the proposition that all men are created equal.

Now we are engaged in a great civil war, testing whether that nation, or any nation so conceived and so dedicated, can long endure. We are met on a great battle-field of that war. We have come to dedicate a portion of that field, as a final resting place for those who here gave their lives that that nation might live. It is altogether fitting and proper that we should do this.

But, in a larger sense, we can not dedicate—we can not consecrate—we can not hallow—this ground. The brave men, living and dead, who struggled here, have consecrated it, far above our poor power to add or detract. The world will little note, nor long remember what we say here, but it can never forget what they did here. It is for us the living, rather, to be dedicated here to the unfinished work which they who fought here have thus far so nobly advanced. It is rather for us to be here dedicated to the great task remaining before us—that from these honored dead we take increased devotion to that cause for which they gave the last full measure of devotion—that we here highly resolve that these dead shall not have died in vain—that this nation, under God, shall have a new birth of freedom—and that government of the people, by the people, for the people, shall not perish from the earth.

Plain Text Version

What do we need to know and do as readers to understand this text in its simplicity?

Eighty-seven years ago, our ancestors started a new nation based on the idea that all people should be free and equal.

Now we are fighting a civil war to see if such a nation can last. Today we meet to honor those buried on this battlefield. It is right to do this.

It's not up to us to make this an important place. Those who fought and died here have already done that. No one will remember what is said here, but many will remember what they did here. It is up to us to finish the work the soldiers began. We must commit to this challenge so their deaths have meaning. This nation should remain free and this form of government shall survive.

Overdone Example

What do we need to know and do as readers to understand this text in its extravagance?

Four score and seven years ago, our future-thinking forefathers fought to bring forth a foundling nation conceived to foster liberty and dedicated to the ultimate essential principle of freedom for all—that all people—every single person in the nation—are at this moment and shall forevermore remain free.

Now we, the fortunate benefactors of our forefathers' efforts, are involved in a tremendous civil war, the likes of which few here or anywhere else have ever seen before. This war in which we are engaged is testing whether a nation torn asunder but based on the principles set forth by those forefathers can remain as noble and pure as the eagle, that majestic avian being that represents our union.

Generalization Example

What do we need to know and do as readers to understand this text in its brevity?

Forty-seven years ago, our nation was founded on the concept that all people should be free. Today we are in a terrible civil war because this concept is worth dying for.

Despite its challenges, the original Gettysburg Address text offers the reader more for his or her efforts than any of the other versions. The plain text version, though fairly simple, also seems rather insipid and—to use a dreaded term—b-o-r-i-n-g. The overdone example is too flowery and, as a result, tends to cloak the meaning in too many layers. The abruptness of the generalization example loses almost everything of worth from the original, particularly the impact of its message.

Activities

Impact of Word Choice and Phrasing

Clearly, the beauty of our historical documents needs to be heard in the heads of twenty-first-century learners—to be appreciated by them for the masterful writing and thinking that went into them. Consider the focus in this craft example from the CCSS:

CCSS.ELA-Literacy.RI.11-12.6: Determine an author's point of view or purpose in a text in which the rhetoric is particularly effective, **analyzing how style and content contribute to the power, persuasiveness or beauty of the text.**

The passage below, from a juvenile literature biography of Franklin Delano Roosevelt, helps to show us how a writer can capture emotion in words to aid the reader in understanding a critical event. The writer's craft in this piece creates an emotional tone that allows the reader to develop a mental picture of the tension of a moment that led the American people to develop an appreciation for the strength and resiliency of FDR.

In this piece, the subject has an emotional tone, but the close-analysis activity could also address how the text focuses on curiosity, suspense, surprise, humor, sadness ... the list goes on. If a reader can identify emotional tone, etc., then he or she is more awake to the word choice the author uses to convey a concept. When we create readers who are sensitive to craft, they are more awake to the connections that can become clear—for example, when we start reading a text with many words associated with religion, then we might start looking for why, and generally there will be a connection.

Author's Craft in Roosevelt Speech

Activity: Examine the passage for word choice, wording, sentence structure, and any other elements of the author's craft that heighten its message to answer the question "How does the crafting of this paragraph impact the message?" Then fill out the chart on page 46, either using the suggested elements or identifying others in a new chart.

> "Roosevelt's 16-year-old son James helped his father get around at the convention, which was held in New York. When the time came for Roosevelt to speak, James helped him to the stage. Once there, however, Roosevelt shunned any more help. With the use of his braces and crutches, he crossed the stage on his own. The crowd watched in silence as Roosevelt, with sweat trickling down his forehead, made his way to the podium. Once there, he smiled and waved to the audience. Camera flashbulbs twinkled. The crowd burst into applause and rose in a standing ovation. Roosevelt's speech didn't gain Smith the Democratic nomination for president, which went to former congressman and ambassador John W. Davis. But the speech made Roosevelt famous. Many newspapers even declared Roosevelt should have been nominated for president. In time, he would be."
>
> from *Franklin Delano Roosevelt: The New Deal President* by Brenda Haugen (Compass Point Books, 2006, p. 59).

Impact on Meaning Chart

Text	Impact on Meaning
Roosevelt's … son James <u>helped</u> his father	
get around	
James <u>helped</u> him	
<u>shunned</u> any more help	
his braces and crutches	
on his own	
<u>crowd</u> watched in silence	
sweat trickling down his forehead	
made his way	
once there	
smiled and waved	
flashbulbs twinkled	
<u>crowd</u>	
<u>burst</u> into applause	
<u>rose</u> in a standing ovation	
In time, he would be.	

Sample Answers

Text	Impact on Meaning
Roosevelt's ... son James <u>helped</u> his father	*Mentioning that the son helped his father places emphasis on Roosevelt's infirmity.*
get around	*Using the term "get around," something we accept as a basic capability, also intensifies his weakness.*
James <u>helped</u> him	*Again, the son helps the father, who must rely on help.*
<u>shunned</u> any more help	*The word "shunned" provides an abrupt break from the established pattern. From this point on, Roosevelt accepts no "help."*
his braces and crutches	*He relies on no person but can walk across the stage with only mechanical assistance.*
on his own	*This phrase, not really necessary, intensifies the idea that he crossed the stage without help.*
<u>crowd</u> watched in silence	*Using "crowd" rather than "audience" tends to suggest a larger group—yet they were "silent," nearly impossible for a large group. The reader begins to understand the emotional intensity of what happened that night.*
sweat trickling down his forehead	*Mentioning this detail emphasizes the cost to Roosevelt of this demonstration of independence.*
made his way	*Using this expression tends to suggest more difficulty than "walked."*
once there	*This highlights his arrival, particularly because it is not really necessary for meaning.*
smiled and waved	*Mentioning these actions demonstrates how calm Roosevelt chooses to appear and contrasts with the effort he has just expended crossing the stage.*
flashbulbs twinkled	*That the flashbulbs "twinkle" creates a cheerful mood—a celebration.*
<u>crowd</u>	*Again, "crowd" tends to suggest a larger group than "audience."*
<u>burst</u> into applause	*Choosing "burst" strengthens the intensity of the crowd's reaction for the reader.*
<u>rose</u> in a standing ovation	*"Rose" suggests a unified action in response to Roosevelt's successful arrival.*
In time, he would be.	*This short, simple sentence calmly lays out Roosevelt's future, as if this event decided the presidency. The overall impact is to intensify Roosevelt's achievement.*

SIDENOTE—Gerri: I am a dedicated reader of fiction, and I have always enjoyed my professional reading, yet for years, other nonfiction works seldom drew my attention. Then I picked up *Fuzzy Thinking* by Bart Kosko, the first nonfiction book I approached the way I attack a good novel: I devoured it. I could hardly wait to get home each night to pick up the book again. Why? The subject, certainly, but Kosko, like Sapolsky, writes engaging text—and tells a good story along the way. The elegant simplicity of his lead sentence for the first chapter models for us just what a careful author can do to draw the reader into his text through his story.

Understanding the Author's Craft: JFK Inaugural Address

Background

In addressing the theme of global citizenship, political leaders carry great weight. Just what makes some of them—Winston Churchill, Abraham Lincoln, Margaret Thatcher, Tony Blair, Charles de Gaulle, Franklin Delano Roosevelt, John F. Kennedy—more successful in persuading others to ally with their cause? Generally, they understand the importance of the crafting of their message, and they wield an author's tools skillfully to present a message that convinces the audience. An astute reader will recognize the craft components that work together to convey the writer's ideas and grasp the entire meaning.

Just what does this mean for the audience? The pairing of John F. Kennedy and Robert Frost serves as a metaphor for the marriage of informational text and strategies often seen in narration. Frost wrote to Kennedy about the promises of the combined impact of poetry and power (Academy). Kennedy responded: "It's poetry and power all the way!" (Academy). This section of the craft chapter will show that Kennedy and his advisor/speech writer Ted Sorensen, both skillful writers, drew on adept use of rhetoric, but also relied on the storyteller's arsenal to enhance their informational text. A careful reader will utilize those strategies to unlock meaning by understanding how Kennedy developed it.

Often authors begin with a review of what others have done before them. Kennedy chose to survey what factors resulted in success for the writings of others and asked Ted Sorensen to review successful inaugural speeches and Lincoln's Gettysburg Address to determine what characteristics they had in common (Department of Education and Public Programs, "Analyzing the Inaugural Address," 2). He also sought input from others, among them Adlai Stevenson and John Kenneth Galbraith. Kennedy and Sorensen then utilized insights and text bits from this survey in writing JFK's own highly regarded inaugural address (Department of Education and Public Programs, "Analyzing the Rhetoric of JFK's Inaugural Address," 1). The resulting text is complex, yet effective and rewards the careful reader with skillfully developed morsels of meaning.

When readers are more aware of or awake to author's craft, they are less likely to be manipulated by it. By helping students read with an awareness of craft, we are helping them become citizens who can appreciate craft but not be manipulated by it.

JFK Inaugural Address Example

To continue our focus on what it means to be a citizen of the world and of the United States of America, let's consider an excerpt from JFK's inaugural address in which he focused the nation on "the common enemies of man: tyranny, poverty, disease, and war itself," asking "what together we can do for the freedom of man" (Kennedy). The speech fits our theme, but it also models what powerful text can do—and ***shows us how an author creates an intended message by utilizing the author's craft.*** Despite its brevity, it shines as one of the greatest inaugural addresses, echoing the impact of Lincoln's Gettysburg Address.

Just how did Kennedy accomplish so much in such a brief text? First, he knew that his message would be important, because he had won the popular vote by a small margin and wanted to build that margin into confidence in his presidency—which he did. After his address, "nearly seventy-five percent of Americans expressed approval of President Kennedy" (Department of Education and Public Programs, "Analyzing the Inaugural Address," 3). Second, he wisely realized the power of a well-written speech.

Kennedy's speech, according to a BBC article written by Max Atkinson, drew on the use of contrast, three-part lists, alliteration, and "bold imagery" (Atkinson 1), as well as other rhetorical devices for its impact. Clearly, "*How* does the text say it?" is a key question in understanding the Kennedy address, so we'll analyze aspects of an excerpt from the address.

JFK Inaugural Address Conclusion

In your hands, my fellow citizens, more than mine, will rest the final success or failure of our course. Since this country was founded, each generation of Americans has been summoned to give testimony to its national loyalty. The graves of young Americans who answered the call to service surround the globe.

Now the trumpet summons us again—not as a call to bear arms, though arms we need—not as a call to battle, though embattled we are—but a call to bear the burden of a long twilight struggle, year in and year out, "rejoicing in hope, patient in tribulation"—a struggle against the common enemies of man: tyranny, poverty, disease and war itself.

Can we forge against these enemies a grand and global alliance, North and South, East and West, that can assure a more fruitful life for all mankind? Will you join in that historic effort?

In the long history of the world, only a few generations have been granted the role of defending freedom in its hour of maximum danger. I do not shrink from this responsibility—I welcome it. I do not believe that any of us would exchange places with any other people or any other generation. The energy, the faith, the devotion which we bring to this endeavor will light our country and all who serve it—and the glow from that fire can truly light the world.

continued —

And so, my fellow Americans: ask not what your country can do for you—ask what you can do for your country.

My fellow citizens of the world: ask not what America will do for you, but what together we can do for the freedom of man.

Finally, whether you are citizens of America or citizens of the world, ask of us here the same high standards of strength and sacrifice which we ask of you. With a good conscience our only sure reward, with history the final judge of our deeds, let us go forth to lead the land we love, asking His blessing and His help, but knowing that here on earth God's work must truly be our own (Department of Education and Public Programs, "Analyzing the Inaugural Address").

Approximate Lexile Level: 1220

The question "How does the text create meaning?" calls for an examination of the craft and structure of the text and consequently corresponds to the College and Career Readiness Anchor Standards 4, 5, and 6, respectively. Although a quick survey of online analyses reveals that classical rhetoric plays a strong role in Kennedy's speech, we will explore the speech without a tour through anaphora, anastrophe, or any of their cousins, although several are present in the speech. In no way do we intend this to be a thorough analysis of Kennedy's speech, which deserves (and has received) far more attention than we give it here. For those interested in curricular materials that probe the speech in further detail, we recommend the teacher resources at the John F. Kennedy Presidential Library and Museum.

Walk Through: Common Core State Reading Standards 4, 5, and 6

Now let's explore the excerpt from Kennedy's inaugural address by dipping into standards 4, 5, and 6.

CCSS: Craft and Structure

How does the text say it?

4. Interpret words and phrases as they are used in a text, including determining technical, connotative, and figurative meanings, and analyze how specific word choices shape meaning or tone.
5. Analyze the structure of texts, including how specific sentences, paragraphs, and larger portions of the text (e.g., a section, chapter, scene, or stanza) relate to each other and the whole.
6. Assess how point of view or purpose shapes the content and style of a text.

4. CCSS.ELA-Literacy.CCRA.R.4—Interpret words and phrases as they are used in a text, including determining technical, connotative, and figurative meanings, and analyze how specific word choices shape meaning or tone.

This excerpt from J.F. Kennedy's inaugural address presents many opportunities for a careful analysis to unlock deeper meaning. For example, "...each generation of Americans has been summoned to give testimony to its national loyalty," clearly lays out the idea that every generation of Americans has had to prove its patriotism. However, the next sentence strikes a far stronger chord with "the graves of young Americans" that "surround the globe." Kennedy's exchange of the abstract nature of "loyalty" for the tragic reality of "the graves of young Americans" intensifies the impact of his message. Having those graves "surround the globe," edges into hyperbole, yet it carries the seeds of truth, for many Americans have lost their lives in distant lands.

The conclusion contains the lines that are among the most-quoted of all of Kennedy's words: "...ask not what your country can do for you—ask what you can do for your country." What makes these words resonate so strongly in our minds? Part of their impact lies in the message, but the word order and word choice make them far more powerful. For example, had JFK said, "Don't ask how your country can help you. Instead, ask how you can help your country," would the listening nation have remembered those words? No, as there is little that is memorable about this version. Beginning with a reversal of normal order ("Ask not" instead of "Don't ask"), Kennedy captures our attention and maintains it with the contrasting elements hanging on either side of the dash and by changing the position of "you" from passive recipient to doer.

Kennedy's entire address provides fertile ground for mining of figurative language, sound devices, and rhetorical elements. The John F. Kennedy Library and Museum supplies a worksheet titled "Analyzing the Rhetoric of JFK's Inaugural Address" that has a section called "Rhetorical Terms and Techniques of Persuasion" with 13 different rhetorical terms and examples of their use drawn from the speech (Department of Education and Public Programs). See the mine maps later in this chapter for our additional work with the excerpt.

5. CCSS.ELA-Literacy.CCRA.R.5—Analyze the structure of texts, including how specific sentences, paragraphs, and larger portions of the text (e.g., a section, chapter, scene, or stanza) relate to each other and the whole.

This small portion of the entire address has an observable structure, and it fits tightly into the larger whole, although we would need to see the entire text to demonstrate that. Even examining just the conclusion, however, can provide us with a view of the careful organization of the speech. The concluding section begins with a key to the message: Kennedy is soliciting a commitment from every American, for he opens by telling his listeners that the success of his course of action rests "in [their] hands." The first paragraph reminds his audience of the terrible price of loyalty paid by Americans before us. The second paragraph tells us that we are "summon[ed]" again, only the fight is a broader one against "the common enemies of man." Next, he asks two key questions: "Can we...?" and "Will you join...?" He answers the questions himself in the next paragraph by reminding listeners of the significance of defending "freedom in its hour of maximum danger" and assuring us that he "welcome[s]" the responsibility—definitely a comforting thought for Americans contemplating the fright of the Cold War ahead. Then the speech drops in the rhetorical bomb, asking Americans to join in the struggle, committing to what they can "do for [their] country" and "for the freedom of man." At the conclusion of the excerpt and the speech, he reminds his audience that "a good conscience" will serve as their "reward" and that God is on their side, for "here on earth God's work must truly be our own." There is a religious motif here—"final judge," "trumpet," "sacrifice," etc. Kennedy's challenge was likely intended to tap into religious beliefs: "...asking His blessing and His help, but knowing that here on earth God's work must truly be our own."

Looking at the first few words of each paragraph gives us a clue to the carefully orchestrated structure:

Role of Initial Words/Transitions

Activity: Have students identify the role of each item in the first column of the chart.

Initial Words/Transitions	Role
"In your hands"	Enlist commitment from the audience
"Now"	Place emphasis on the immediacy of the issue
"Can we" and "Will you"	Introduce the key questions
"In the long history of the world"	Heighten the significance of the requested commitment
"And so, my fellow Americans"	Lead into the power message by identifying with the audience
"My fellow citizens of the world"	Broaden the audience to global citizenship
"Finally"	Conclude

6. **CCSS.ELA-Literacy.CCRA.R.6—Assess how point of view or purpose shapes the content and style of a text.**

*Kennedy relied on first- and second-person points of view to personalize his message, as he won the election by a narrow margin of the popular vote and needed to elicit support from his listeners. His inaugural address helped listening Americans establish confidence in their new, young Catholic President. Using first-person pronouns throughout, particularly at key points at which he requested commitment from the audience, helped to place him with them in the struggle ahead rather than over it. Saying "**I** do not shrink from this responsibility—**I** welcome it" suggests to the audience that this is a man who is committing himself to direct involvement. The warmth of "My fellow Americans," which so many other presidents have favored, comes largely from the first-person "My" juxtaposed with "fellow."*

*Second person also appears in carefully selected sections, as listeners' support will come only if they see America's battle in the Cold War as their struggle. Thus, the conclusion opens by placing the success of "**our** course" "in **your** hands...more than **mine**" (emphasis added.) The point of view moves from first-person plural to second person to first-person singular. The resulting impact: listeners see themselves as needing to commit to the difficult times ahead, yet they will have the support of an involved, committed leader along the way.*

Performance Task Activities

Activity: Perspective in Kennedy's Inaugural Address

John F. Kennedy had a viewpoint that was in many ways unique among presidents: He was new, young, and Catholic. Reread the segment of his inaugural address and discuss how that perspective may have influenced his speech. Use specific evidence from the speech to support your ideas.

Activity: Analysis of Kennedy's Use of the Author's Craft

Once the students have analyzed the text using the standards identified previously, they could be asked to construct a response explaining how Kennedy and his speech writers used craft to enhance his message. The chart from the Kennedy Library that shows changes from Galbraith's and Stevenson's suggested text to the versions that appear in the final draft ("Excerpts from Inaugural Suggestions and Delivered Speech") may be useful here. It is another section of the longer document "Analyzing the Rhetoric of JFK's Inaugural Address" (Department of Education and Public Programs). This activity could easily become a performance task.

Text-dependent Questions

Laying the Groundwork: Understandings/Key Ideas of the Text

The ACHIEVE group has developed teacher resources for working with text-dependent questions and published them on a website with "Steal These Tools" as the home page heading. We have gratefully accepted their offer and used their guidelines for the numbered items in the next section. Please see the "Works Cited" page at the end of the chapter for ACHIEVE (Student Achievement Partners) information.

Both teachers and students profit heavily from identifying key ideas and understandings of a text. Whether highlighting the ideas or rewording them in a list, getting a solid feeling for the key ideas helps focus on the main message and its development. For example, in the JFK inaugural address conclusion, we began with highlighting the most significant ideas and then listed them before working on deeper-level text-dependent questions. See Chapter Two for additional material on the ACHIEVE process for developing text-dependent questions. Chapter Three focuses on craft, so the text-dependent questions here examine the text by analyzing, synthesizing, or evaluating the text for author's craft topics (e.g., vocabulary, text structure, author's purpose, etc).

John F. Kennedy brings out several key ideas in this conclusion to his inaugural address:

- *He places the responsibility for success or failure of America's course of action in the hands of its people.*
- *He speaks of a call to action against four "enemies of man": tyranny, poverty, disease, and war.*
- *He asks if America can create a major worldwide alliance to fight these enemies.*
- *He reminds his audience that they are defending freedom at its most perilous time.*
- *In order for all of this to happen, Americans must look not for what they can receive from their country, but instead what they can do for it, and he echoes the same idea in a global thrust for the independence of mankind.*
- *He closes with a suggestion that this is God's work and that he and other Americans will be acting out of love for their country.*

What is the main message John F. Kennedy suggests in this concluding section of his inaugural address?

He asks his fellow Americans if they can create a major worldwide alliance to fight the "enemies of man" (tyranny, poverty, disease, and war) to make the lives of all men everywhere more productive. ("Can we forge against these enemies a grand and global alliance, North and South, East and West, which can assure a more fruitful life for all mankind?")

1. Orientation/Confidence Building

What strategies does JFK use to help his audience feel as though he is one of them and speaking directly to each person in his audience?

He speaks to them in a direct address technique using "my fellow citizens," "my fellow Americans," and "my fellow citizens of the world." By referring to the audience as "my fellow _____," he suggests that he is one of them—an equal. For most people, hearing that the president is your "fellow American" tends to be somewhat heartwarming. Using first person (I, my, our) and second person (you, your) increases the sense of immediacy and involvement. A third-person narration or speech tends to be objective and somewhat cold.

2. Vocabulary and Text Structure

What words seem to have a particularly significant impact on Kennedy's key ideas?

By choosing to refer to his audience as "my fellow citizens," "my fellow Americans," and "my fellow citizens of the world," he increases the likelihood of engaging them, as these expressions have a rather appealing warmth—so much so that many succeeding presidents frequently used "my fellow Americans."

His call to action uses "burden" and "struggle," both of which carry a message of extended troubles in the days ahead. "Burden" suggests a heavy, ever-present load, and "struggle" tends to suggest an ongoing conflict. He apparently wanted Americans to realize that the battle to which he called them would present an immense challenge, but he does not suggest a war-level involvement. A struggle, though definitely a fight, tends not to carry the implications of heavy combat.

The glory of a "grand and global alliance" tends to suggest a majestic quality for the partnership he wished to form. "Grand" seems to carry a tinge of glory or magnificence on an almost royal scale. Kennedy wished for his listeners to feel the power of what he suggested—not a simple global conference, but an impressive worldwide coalition.

To name the goal of this alliance, Kennedy chose "freedom," a term that has special significance for every American, as it provides the foundation for our country's existence.

"In its hour of maximum danger" draws on a potent emotion—fear—to intensify his message. Suggesting that our country is in great peril places considerable emphasis on the importance of Kennedy's call to arms.

3. Tough Sections

What is the meaning of "a long twilight struggle" in the following section of the conclusion?

> "Now the trumpet summons us again—not as a call to bear arms, though arms we need—not as a call to battle, though embattled we are—but a call to bear the burden of a long twilight struggle, year in and year out, 'rejoicing in hope, patient in tribulation'—a struggle against the common enemies of man: tyranny, poverty, disease and war itself."

Kennedy is suggesting that the work ahead does not have a quick, simple solution. Instead, he wants his audience to know that long-term, consistent exertion will be the only way to win this fight. Note that he stops short of calling it a battle or suggesting war. "Twilight" is an interesting addition to "struggle," for it carries with it the double implications of a time at which the daylight hours have already accomplished the bulk of the tasks for the day and the hours ahead are dark and unknown. The struggle the American people were entering was to be long, less intense than armed conflict, and at a point at which the future was unknown.

Activities

Mining Maps

Development of knowledge of the craft and structure of the text. This kind of analysis called for in the Common Core State Reading Standards is difficult for students. The craft and structure maps in Appendix 3a assist students in their analysis. The following activity could be used to give students support in doing this type of close inspection of the text.

Small-group analysis of text. Have students reading/viewing the same text on the ELMO or screen, and have tables/mining maps listing imagery/figures of speech. (See the table on page 56 and Appendix 3a.) The teacher asks for these by name, and the table captain raises her hand and offers the find. Or the teacher asks each table to identify how many of the different types of imagery/figures of speech have been found and calls on tables to respond. Table captains do not repeat what has been found by other tables but simply add to the list.

Imagery/Figures of Speech
1. Simile 2. Metaphor: *"twilight struggle," "light our country," "the glow from that fire," "light the world"* 3. Personification: *"trumpet summons"* 4. Alliteration: *"more than mine," "service surround," "bear the burden," "grand and global," "standards of strength and sacrifice," "lead the land we love,"* 5. Onomatopoeia 6. Allusion 7. Satire/Parody 8. Exaggeration/Hyperbole: *"graves...surround the globe"* 9. Irony/Sarcasm 10. Repetition/Omission: *"—not as a call to bear arms, though arms we need—not as a call to battle, though embattled we are," "twilight struggle...struggle against," "I do not shrink from...I do not believe," "ask not what...ask what," "citizens of America or citizens of the world," "ask of us...we ask of you," "His blessing...His help"* 11. Symbolism: *"trumpet"* 12. Oxymoron 13. Over-/Understatement 14. Motif 15. Intertextuality: *"trumpet summons us"* (biblical references to trumpet call) 16. Language: precise, formal/scholarly with literary elements, scientific

The same activity can be done with the other mining maps, such as the writer's craft map.

The Depth-of-Knowledge level for this activity would be under "analysis" at the DOK Level 3.

Writer's Craft: Writing Techniques
1. Lead: *"In your hands, my fellow citizens, more than mine, will rest the final success or failure of our course."* 2. Use of statistics 3. Professional/scientific vocabulary/domain-specific/nomenclature (e.g., Latin and Greek) and also foreign words: *"tyranny, poverty, disease and war itself," "alliance," "freedom"* 4. Technical vocabulary 5. Quoting experts, citing books, articles, journals; Biblical Quotation: *"rejoicing in hope, patient in tribulation"* (King James Version, Romans 12.12) 6. Precise/detailed examples in proof 7. Examples chosen for audience appeal/interest: *"The graves of young Americans who answered the call to service surround the globe." "In the long history of the world, only a few generations have been granted the role of defending freedom in its hour of maximum danger." "Let us go forth to lead the land we love...."* 8. Explanation, description, definition, step-by-step how-to: *The first two paragraphs explain the conclusion's lead sentence. Paragraph four ("In the long history") explains the commitments involved.* 9. Varying sentence length and sentence structure: *Short for impact: "Will you join in that historic effort?"* 10. Word choice: *"a long twilight struggle," "a grand and global alliance"* 11. Punctuation for effect (ellipses, parentheses, exclamation points, boldface, italics, dashes for contrasting elements and setting off material)

Hess's Cognitive Rigor Matrix (Hess)

Revised Bloom's Taxonomy	Webb's DOK Level 1 Recall & Reproduction	Webb's DOK Level 2 Basic Skills & Concepts	Webb's DOK Level 3 Strategic Thinking/ Reasoning	Webb's DOK Level 4 Extended Thinking
Analyze	• Identify whether specific information is contained in graphic representations (e.g., map, chart, table, graph, T-chart, diagram,) or text features (e.g., headings, subheadings, captions) • Decide which text structure is appropriate to audience and purpose	• Categorize/ compare literary elements, terms, facts/details, events • Identify use of literary devices • Analyze format, organization, and internal text structure (signal words, transitions, semantic cues) of different texts • Distinguish: relevant-irrelevant information; fact/ opinion • Identify characteristic text features; distinguish between texts, genres	• Analyze information within data sets or texts • Analyze interrelationships among concepts, issues, problems • Analyze or interpret author's craft (literary devise, viewpoint, or potential bias) to create or critique a text • Use reasoning, planning, and evidence to support inferences	• Analyze multiple sources of evidence or multiple works by the same author or across genres, time periods, themes • Analyze complex/ abstract themes, perspectives, concepts • Gather, analyze, and organize multiple information sources • Analyze discourse styles

Craft Card Game Activity

Give each group of students the cards in Appendix 3b and a copy of an informational text. At the beginning of the year/semester, you might provide copies of a text with figurative language examples underlined as support. As students become more familiar with the terms, the underlining is no longer necessary. A student draws a card and looks for an example of the term in the text provided. After an allotted amount of time, identify the examples and students check their work. Discuss any examples that students find that were not the ones you identified.

Guided Highlighted Reading Practice

The GHR activity serves as a helpful tool for giving students practice in working with complex text. Appendix 3c has a short GHR activity for author's craft based on the J.F. Kennedy Inaugural Address text addressed in this chapter. Appendix 3d has a longer GHR activity based on a more challenging Herbert Hoover speech.

The boldfaced text in each standard on page 58 shows the difference in expectation from the previous standard. For the Kennedy Inaugural Address, we would use grades 9 and 10, although the passage has an approximate Lexile level of 1220, which might place it in grade 11 or above.

Standards Progression

Informational Craft and Structure Standards 4.4–12.4
• CSS.ELA-Literacy.RI.4.4: Determine the meaning of general academic and domain-specific words or phrases in a text relevant to a *grade 4 topic or subject area.* • CCSS.ELA-Literacy.RI.5.4: Determine the meaning of general academic and domain-specific words and phrases in a text relevant to a ***grade*** *5 topic or subject area.* • CCSS.ELA-Literacy.RI.6.4: Determine the meaning of words and phrases **as they are used in a text, including figurative, connotative, and technical meanings.** • CCSS.ELA-Literacy.RI.7.4: Determine the meaning of words and phrases as they are used in a text, including figurative, connotative, and technical meanings; **analyze the impact of a specific word choice on meaning and tone.** • CCSS.ELA-Literacy.RI.8.4: Determine the meaning of words and phrases as they are used in a text, including figurative, connotative, and technical meanings; analyze the impact of specific word choices on meaning and tone, **including analogies or allusions to other texts.** • CCSS.ELA-Literacy.RI.9-10.4: Determine the meaning of words and phrases as they are used in a text, including figurative, connotative, and technical meanings; analyze the cumulative impact of specific word choices on meaning and tone **(e.g., how the language of a court opinion differs from that of a newspaper).** • CCSS.ELA-Literacy.RI.11-12.4: Determine the meaning of words and phrases as they are used in a text, including figurative, connotative, and technical meanings; **analyze how an author uses and refines the meaning of a key term or terms over the course of a text (e.g., how Madison defines faction in Federalist No. 10).**

Informational Craft and Structure Standards 4.5–12.5
• CCSS.ELA-Literacy.RI.4.5: Describe the overall structure (e.g., chronology, comparison, cause/effect, problem/solution) of events, ideas, concepts, or information in a text or part of a text. • CCSS.ELA-Literacy.RI.5.5: **Compare and contrast the overall structure (e.g., chronology, comparison, cause/effect, problem/solution)** of events, ideas, concepts, or information **in two or more texts.** • CCSS.ELA-Literacy.RI.6.5: **Analyze how a particular sentence, paragraph, chapter, or section fits into the overall structure of a text and contributes to the development of the ideas.** • CCSS.ELA-Literacy.RI.7.5: **Analyze the structure an author uses to organize a text, including how the major sections contribute to the whole and to the development of the ideas.** • CCSS.ELA-Literacy.RI.8.5: Analyze in detail the structure **of a specific paragraph in a text, including the role of particular sentences in developing and refining a key concept.** • CCSS.ELA-Literacy.RI.9-10.5: Analyze in detail **how an author's ideas or claims are developed and refined by particular sentences, paragraphs, or larger portions of a text (e.g., a section or chapter).** • CCSS.ELA-Literacy.RI.11-12.5: Analyze **and evaluate the effectiveness of the structure an author uses in his or her exposition or argument, including whether the structure makes points clear, convincing, and engaging.**

Informational Craft and Structure Standards 4.6–12.6
• CCSS.ELA-Literacy.RI.4.6: Compare and contrast a firsthand and secondhand account of the same event or topic; describe the differences in focus and the information provided. • CCSS.ELA-Literacy.RI.5.6: **Analyze multiple accounts of the same event or topic, noting important similarities and differences in the point of view they represent.** • CCSS.ELA-Literacy.RI.6.6: **Determine an author's point of view or purpose in a text and explain how it is conveyed in the text.** • CCSS.ELA-Literacy.RI.7.6: Determine an author's point of view or purpose in a text and **analyze how the author distinguishes his or her position from that of others.** • CCSS.ELA-Literacy.RI.8.6: Determine an author's point of view or purpose in a text and **analyze how the author acknowledges and responds to conflicting evidence or viewpoints.** • CCSS.ELA-Literacy.RI.9-10.6: Determine an author's point of view or purpose in a text **and analyze how an author uses rhetoric to advance that point of view or purpose.** • CCSS.ELA-Literacy.RI.11-12.6: Determine an author's point of view or purpose in a text **in which the rhetoric is particularly effective, analyzing how style and content contribute to the power, persuasiveness or beauty of the text.**

Student Assessment and Teacher Effectiveness

In these days of expanded focus on proving that students have achieved, data collection has become an exceptionally vital part of every teacher's classroom preparation. Each of us must continually ask and answer the hard questions:

- What should my students learn this semester/year?
- Are my students learning all that they need to learn?
- What data might I collect that will prove how much my students have learned?

In each of our chapters, we try to provide teachers assistance by suggesting material for data collection. These lists are not all-inclusive. Review the standards recommended at the state and/or national level for skills.

Identification of Craft Elements

Count the number of craft elements (figurative, connotative, and technical language elements) identified in a text of grade-level difficulty at the beginning of the semester/year and again at the end of the semester/year. It is possible to use the same text for both pre- and post-tests, but students should not see their papers or reveal any answers until after the second administration of the test at the end of the year.

Multiple-choice or Written Analysis

Write a multiple-choice test addressing text elements from the following list or from the standards as they apply to a text or texts. Another option is to supply students with a text and a writing prompt asking them to analyze how the following components function within the text:

- impact of specific word choice on meaning and tone
- development of ideas in a text
- author's perspective/point of view and purpose
- structure/organization of a text—how ideas develop, including role of specific sentences, paragraphs, and larger passages
- how an author acknowledges and responds to conflicting evidence or viewpoints
- how documents of historical and literary significance address related themes and concepts
- how an author uses and refines the meaning of key terms
- the effectiveness of the style and content of a text

Craft

Our intent in creating this exploration of the author's craft from the reader's perspective is to provide tools for teachers to use in helping students develop the skills necessary to read complex texts. Whether it is mining the text for author's strategies, analyzing a text for its structure, or simply contemplating the implications of selecting one word over another, each experience will deepen students' understanding of how to approach the *next* complex text.

SIDENOTE—Gerri: In my first writing workshop, I heard a statement that has been a keystone of my practice as a writing teacher: "The object is not to make this a better piece of writing. The object is to make this student a better writer." With this in mind, I dropped my red pen and opened my mouth—to ask students questions that encouraged *them* to think about how to develop the text they were creating. I had to learn to stop doing my students' thinking for them.

Turning this around and focusing it as reading advice, I had to learn to stop simply providing my students explications of texts and develop a system for gradually turning over the explication process to the students. How? Yes, begin with the oral explication, but then turn it over to small groups of students, then to partners, and finally, to the individual student. It took me a while to give up control, but when I did, my students became better readers because they, not I, were doing the thinking. *My* thinking came in advance—in deciding when and how to release control to my students as I planned my lessons.

Chapter Three Works Cited

Academy of American Poets. "Poetry and Power: Robert Frost's Inaugural Reading." *POETS.org.* n.d. Web. 24 April 2013.

Atkinson, Max. "JFK's Inaugural Speech: Six Secrets of His Success." *BBC News: US and Canada.* 18 January 2011. Web. 22 April 2013.

Brown, John Russell, and Terence John Bew Spencer, eds. "Shakespeare, William." *Encyclopedia Britannica's Guide to Shakespeare.* 2013. Web. 29 April, 2013.

Department of Education and Public Programs. "Analyzing the Inaugural Address." John F. Kennedy Presidential Library and Museum. n.d. Web. 23 April. 2013.

- - - - - - - - - - - - . "Analyzing the Rhetoric of JFK's Inaugural Address." John F. Kennedy Presidential Library and Museum. n.d. Web. 23 April. 2013.

Frost, Robert. "Stopping by Woods on a Snowy Evening." Quoted in Academy of American Poets. "Poetry and Power: Robert Frost's Inaugural Reading." *POETS.org.* n.d. Web. 24 April 2013.

Grothe, Mardy. "Chiasmus." drmardy.com. n.d. Web. 24 April 2013.

Haugen, Brenda. *Franklin Delano Roosevelt: The New Deal President.* Minneapolis: Compass Point Books, 2006.

Hess, Karen K. "Hess's Cognitive Rigor Matrix." National Center for the Improvement of Educational Assessment. 2011. Web. 13 July 2013.

Kennedy, John F. "Inaugural Address, 20 January, 1961." John F. Kennedy Presidential Library and Museum. n.d. Web. 14 April 2013.

Lincoln, Abraham. "Gettysburg Address." Avalon Project: Documents in Law, History, and Diplomacy. Lillian Goldman Law Library. Yale Law School. 2008. Web. 27 August 2013.

"Robert Browning." *Encyclopedia Britannica.* 2013. Web. 29 April 2013.

Student Achievement Partners (ACHIEVE). "A Guide to Creating Text Dependent Questions for Close Analytic Reading." *Steal These Tools: ELA/Literacy.* n.d. Web. 16 July 2013.

CHAPTER FOUR: **READING VISUAL TEXTS**

Summary: What Does the Text Say?

Initially, one starts with summary, the first building block of comprehension. **What does the text say?**

Students retell just the facts of the visual image—what do they literally see? The teacher may prompt with the following: "I want you to tell me exactly what you see. Do not interpret the visual text; just tell me what you see. We are interested in just the facts."

Initially, the teacher may want to approach this assignment as a classroom activity. The teacher can show the visual text via an LCD projector and take notes of student comments. Or, the teacher could make copies of the picture for the students and then write students' observations on the board.

The teacher may have to draw students' attention to details and facts that they miss. However, before prompting, give students time to read the text. Remember to use wait time. Prior to this assignment, the teacher must read the text at a literal level. Thus, she can prompt the students if they have missed a detail, particularly one that is crucial to further rereading of the visual text for meaning.

Several of the prompts for the visual images in this chapter reference color of the cartoon. For full-color versions of the images, search for "Reading to the Core" online, and click on "Reading to the Core Chapter 4 Visual Texts."

Storyteller's View: Visual Literacy

"I did see, with my own eyes..."

Visual literacy has grown immensely important as we cope with the rush of images speeding before our eyes in any moment during an average day. When shopping, for example, even in the little children's department, how often do we stop and take a serious look at the images on a size 4 T-shirt? Either we do or a child's birthday present might bring with it a message we did not intend. The sexual innuendos in the average advertisement developed for the teen audience have become increasingly blatant. Whether we find the messages acceptable or not, students need to know when visual text is attempting to manipulate them.

The twenty-first century is awash with visual images and texts. Yet, too often we ignore the reading of visual texts due to the pressures of written text assessments. However, the two do not have to be taught separately. The process of reading visual texts is the same as the process of reading written texts, and students need to be conscious of this fact. We want all students to be critical readers of their visual worlds.

Below is a political cartoon entitled "Welcome to All," available through the Library of Congress.

Summary Prompts

Depending on the responses, a teacher may need to prompt for the following:

- What words do you see on the cartoon and where are they displayed? *(On the boat are the words "U.S. Ark of Refuge." Tacked on the side of the boat is a sign that says "Free education. Free land. Free speech. Free ballot. Free lunch." On the shore is a sign that reads "No oppressive taxes. No expensive kings. No compulsory military service, No knouts or dungeons.")*
- What is the title of the cartoon? *("Welcome To All")*
- What word is in the top-right corner of the cartoon, and what shape are the clouds in directly below the word? *(The word is "War," and the clouds look like monsters. There may be some dark birds as well.)*
- What possessions are the people carrying? How do they carry their possessions? *(They have the clothes on their backs, and they carry their possessions in a basket, a satchel, cloth bags, and a bag tied to a stick.)*
- What do you notice about some of the people's feet? *(Some are barefoot, some have boots, and some have shoes/clogs.)*
- What do you notice about some of the people's hats or head coverings? *(There are top hats, fancy hats, scarves, etc.)*
- How many women are entering the ark? How many men are entering the ark? *(Eight men and six women)*
- What is flying to the right of the ark? *(A U.S. flag)*

- What ethnic groups are represented and how many of each? *(All are Caucasian except maybe a Chinese man.)*
- What colors are in the cartoon? *(Black, white, and gray)*
- What is the name of the magazine at the top of the Cartoon? *(Puck)*
- How is the man greeting them dressed, and how is he holding his body? *(The man greeting them is in a top hat, long tails, and a striped vest and pants; his arms are outstretched.)*
- What is the name of the cartoonist? *(Keppler)*

Activity: Four-sentence Summary

As a class, the students could now try to summarize the picture in four sentences, determining what they think is important to include in the summary. Use information from the visual.

The answer might look like the following:
The political cartoon by Keppler, "Welcome to All!," is in Puck magazine and shows men and women lined up in pairs entering the U.S. Ark of Refuge. The men and women are being greeted by a man with a white beard and a tall hat and striped pants. The man greeting them has his arms outstretched. In the background, there are dark clouds in the shapes of monsters, and above them is the word "WAR."

SIDENOTE: A Flint ELA high school teacher noted that the summary aspect of a visual text provides students the opportunity to document author and title and summarize without fear of plagiarizing, as a visual text has nothing to plagiarize when translated into words.

The teacher will have to decide how quickly students can be released from teacher-led group summaries of visual texts. If students quickly grasp the concept, then they should be released to do it independently. If they need more support at the start, it could be done in small groups or in partners. The important component to this activity is that the students learn to SEE the evidence. This means they have to RESEE it and slow down. They will not be able to do a summary with a quick scan of the visual.

How Does the Artist Say It?

Once students can do a summary of the visual text, they are ready for the next step or question: **How does the artist say it?** The craft question is an important one with visual texts. The teacher may have to introduce vocabulary, as often students are unaware of visual craft—for example, symbolism. If we expect students to dig deeper, then we must give them the tools to do so, and the vocabulary of craft is an essential tool. Start with visuals that share vocabulary with written texts—stereotypes, for example.

SIDENOTE—Cynthia: I find that students are adept are seeing motifs in visual texts that are often difficult for them to grasp in written text. With a little scaffolding, after they become proficient in identifying motifs in visual texts, they are able to transfer the newfound skill to written texts.

This next step in reading visual texts may be best to do as a group project. However, students will be able to do this independently by high school if we start weaving visual texts into curriculum at the elementary level. Once more, it is important for a teacher to analyze the text first, prior to introducing the visual texts to students. This allows the teacher to create prompts that can guide students to discover the craft that might go unnoticed otherwise.

Prompts

The teacher might say the following: "Okay, class, we are proficient in summarizing visual texts. So, let's take it to the next level of meaning. How does the cartoonist say it? In other words, what craft techniques does the cartoonist choose to convey his/her message? What are the features that the cartoonist uses?" To scaffold students to this level of proficiency, consider supplying them with a mining map for cartoons located in Appendix 4a.

Depending on the responses, a teacher may need to prompt for the following:

- What identifiable symbols does the cartoonist use? *(Uncle Sam, American Flag)*
- Identify the tone the artist creates and support your choice with evidence. *(The cartoonist's attitude toward the subject is sympathetic, given the poverty of the characters and the evil of the winds, but possibly somewhat cynical based on the word choice "free lunch.")*
- What stereotypes does the cartoonist use? *(The clothes of the Chinese man, the nose of the Dutch man and his wife in her clogs, the reserved faces of the wealthier couple)*
- How does the cartoonist use color, and what point is the cartoonist making with his use of color? *(Dark is used to foreshadow or evoke a sense of danger or evil.)*
- How does the author use proximity to convey a point? *(War is shown right over the image of the dark clouds.)*
- Is there any picture or image that conveys metaphoric language? *(Winds of war)*
- How does the author use words? *(The signs emphasize the freedom of the United States.)*
- Why did the cartoonist give a title? *(To emphasize the point or message)*
- Does the cartoon allude to another text? *(It can refer to "Give me your tired, your poor..." in the poem "The New Colossus," by Emma Lazarus.)*
- Does the author use repetition? *(The words "No" and "Free")*
- What mood does the cartoonist create? *(The situation's atmosphere or the characters' feelings are optimistic.)*

- How does the cartoonist create this mood? *(The artist uses less shading in the foreground images than in the background, where the immigrants' origins lie. Uncle Sam's open arms suggest a warm welcome to those starting their lives in a new country far from home. The menacing figures in the clouds contrast sharply with the open arms, supplying reason for optimism.)*
- What words or images don't you know that you think might be important? *("Knout" means "heavy whip.")*
- What is the geographical setting? *(Europe; the immigrants all appear to be from Europe, and the words "No Expensive Kings" support that assumption.)*
- What is the temporal setting? *(The clothes suggest the late 1800s or early 1900s, but given war and Europe, the likely time period seems to be closer to 1914–1918.)*
- What is the socioeconomic status of the people, and how does the cartoonist convey this to the audience? *(The economic status is probably poor, given the lack of possessions and the bare feet, etc.)*
- According to the cartoonist, how does America feel about the immigrants? *(The United States is welcoming them, given the word choice of "Refuge" and Uncle Sam's outstretched, welcoming hands. Plus in the title "Welcome to All!" The exclamation point emphasizes joy emphatically.)*
- What biblical allusion is there in the cartoon? *(Noah's Ark)*

The following chart was created to support students as they develop independence in analyzing the craft of the cartoonist. The chart is also available in Appendix 4a.

Mining the Potential of the Text: Political Cartoon

TEXT STRUCTURE—Power to evoke laughter as well as humiliation; use of comedy to make readers think and draw connections/make a point				
Genre	**Organization**	**Point of View**	**Tone/Mood**	**Text Features**
Editorial cartoon Political cartoon Humor cartoon Animated cartoon	Setting—geographical: local, state, national, international Setting—temporal Setting—social Single panel = cartoon Series of panels = text strip (comic strip)	Bird's-eye view—view from a high angle as if from a bird's vantage point Point of view of cartoonist Political viewpoint	Sarcastic Biting Cynical Satirical	Thought balloons Narration blocks Labels Captions Signs Layout and design: Border Gutters Open panel Panel Splash panel

<table>
<tr><th colspan="10">TEXT STRUCTURE—Power to evoke laughter as well as humiliation; use of comedy to make readers think and draw connections/make a point</th></tr>
<tr><th colspan="2">Genre</th><th colspan="2">Organization</th><th colspan="2">Point of View</th><th colspan="2">Tone/Mood</th><th colspan="2">Text Features</th></tr>
<tr><th colspan="10">AUTHOR'S CRAFT</th></tr>
<tr><th colspan="5">Imagery/Figures of Speech via Visual</th><th colspan="5">Cartoon Techniques</th></tr>
<tr><td colspan="5">Symbols (for example, an elephant represents the Republican Party and a donkey represents the Democratic Party)
Common symbol or image as metaphor
Current events as visual metaphors
Stereotypes
Prejudices
Allegory
Opposing points of view
Objects or characters as symbols
Significant words or phrases
Caricature that parodies the individual
Allusion—indirect reference to past or current event which creates the situation or context into which the individual is placed
Facial expressions
Attire
Body expression and appearance
Recognizable event
Color—symbolic meaning</td><td colspan="5">Cynical—convey scorn or negativity or skepticism
Satirical—use wit to convey insults
Oversimplified opinions through stereotypes
Caricature—exaggeration of personal characteristics to attack a particular person
Satire—use of sarcasm or irony to make fun of somebody or of some event</td></tr>
<tr><td colspan="10">Note: Author and Magazine Published in and date?</td></tr>
</table>

Once students begin to acquire the skill of reading craft, they are ready for the next question: **What does the text mean? (What message/theme/concept is the author trying to get across?)** Once more, the visual text provides opportunities that are not so apparent in written texts. Through a series of questions one can lead students to the core, the meaning of the text. Students can use both literal evidence and craft evidence to support their message/theme/concept. The following questions may help the teacher lead the student to the core:

- Who or what is not present in the cartoon? *(There are no ethnic groups that are dark, nor are there any children. There are no pets; there is no sun, just dark clouds; and there are no old people.)*
- What bothers you about the cartoon and why? *(I am struck by the fact that there are no women who are traveling alone and that the Chinese man apparently does not have a wife and is at the end of the line.)*

- If you could do research for this cartoon, what information would help you understand the cartoon? *(I think if I could research Puck and the cartoonist and his era and political persuasion, then I would have a greater understanding of his intent or message.)*
- What idea appears to be repeating itself? *(Immigrants journeying to America are emphasized by the U.S. Ark of Refuge, the people lined up outside two-by-two, the American flag flying by the ark, and the winds of war at the immigrants' backs. That immigrants are welcomed in America is supported by Uncle Sam's outstretched hands and the caption "WELCOME TO ALL!" Darkness versus light is supported by the darkness of European skies and the lightness of the skies ahead of the ark.)*

Activities for Multiple Meanings

Now the teacher must impress on the students that there is more than one meaning in the text. However, the meaning must be supported from the evidence in the text. There are several classroom activities that could scaffold students on their journey toward meaning.

- Have students rename or name the text. For example, the visual text "WELCOME TO ALL!" could be renamed "Looking for a Few Good Immigrants."
- Have students create a greeting card that would capture the message of the text. Remember a message should transcend the text and be applicable to other texts. For example, you create a card with the word "Welcome" on the cover and pictures of American symbols (e.g., an American flag, the Statue of Liberty, the Liberty Bell, etc.). Then when you open the card, it could state the following: "Congratulations! You fit the bill, and it has benefits." Then you could surround the words with images of the benefits of America.
- Or, ask students to select which image the visual is more like. For example, is this text more like a melting pot or more like a beef stew? Have students defend their selection/choice.
- Or, have students write the message of this text in six words.

No matter what activity, students must be able to defend their stance with evidence from the visual text.

So, what does this mean to me? Message is a natural lead to the final question: **So, what?** Students need to take their learning and transfer it to their lives and other texts. Teachers can ask:

- What does the message/theme/concept mean in your life and/or in the lives of others?
- Why is it worth sharing/telling?
- What significance does it have to your life and/or in the lives of others?

The answers will vary greatly but should relate directly to the message students have determined.

Creating Text-dependent Questions for Visual Texts

Text-dependent questions are a crucial component of expanding students' thinking and reading skills. Douglas Fisher and Nancy Frey's article, "Text-Dependent Questions: Effective Questions About Literature and Nonfiction Texts Require Students to Delve into a Text to Find Answers," can easily be applied to visual texts and *should* be applied to visual texts, as their questions are based upon the Common Core Standards in English language arts. Fisher and Frey encourage a building block of six questions. They start with general understanding questions and scaffold students to opinion, arguments, and intertextual connection questions. The following section applies the six questions to a visual text.

Nurturing students' reading of visual texts takes a great deal of practice. Often the title of a painting is a great way to start to explore the gist of the text. The painting below by Mary Tolliver is titled *Out of the Box*. A full-color version is available online, following the directions listed on page 62. One could ask the following questions to start to reach a general understanding:

General Understanding Questions

- What is the author claiming with the title? In other words, what concepts or words does the phrase evoke? *(creative thinking, nonconformity)*
- What would be the opposite of thinking out of the box? *(boxed in, reduced choices, conformity)*
- How does the text support your word choice/concepts? *(The other eggs are boxed in and appear to be the same size, e.g., conformity, whereas, the one egg is outside the box; it is larger and a different color.)*
- Is there justification for saying that the artist is claiming that being out of the box is nonconformist and offers opportunities that do not exist within the carefully segmented walls? *(Support for this claim could lie in the size of the egg outside the box, which is larger and may suggest that being outside the box provides opportunities for growth not available within the constraints of the box. The outside egg is also lighter and brighter than the others, which are of similar shape, level of brightness, and somewhat subdued color.)*

Key Detail Questions

The next layer of text-dependent questions involves key ideas. These questions focus on important details the author uses (often they can be reached by asking *who, what, where, when, why,* or *how*) to clarify her message. For example, consider the painting *Out of the Box.*

- What is different about the egg outside the box? *(It is larger, and it is a different color.)* This question is a key to understanding the artist's perspective.
- What is the difference between the eggs inside of the box and outside of the box? *(The eggs in the box are smaller and colored, with some matching in color, and all are resting upon soft straw. The large egg rests upon a hard surface, is white, and is not constrained by the walls surrounding the other eggs. Just as the outside egg is separated from the other eggs, so too are the eggs in the box separated.)*

Key detail questions can lead students to insight about the text as the questions focus the reader to specific information that is critical to understanding the text. Furthermore, *key* details, not just details, can scaffold students to a deeper understanding of a text's complexity.

Vocabulary and Text Structure Questions

An author's word choice and text structure are carefully selected. Consequently, vocabulary and text structure questions are critical to understanding the author's message. Vocabulary includes both denotations (definitions) and connotations (ideas or feelings evoked) of words. Vocabulary questions can include figurative language and idioms; vocabulary questions can also provide students an opportunity to use context and structure clues to determine the meaning of unknown words or an artist's choice of colors. For example, consider the painting *Out of the Box.*

- An idiom is a group of words that have meaning beyond the literal words. In other words, the words express a concept beyond the literal meaning. The phrase "out of the box" is an idiom. Why do you think the artist drew it literally? *(Perhaps to juxtapose the concept with the literal.)* How does it impact tone? *(Drawing the idiom literally adds a humorous tone.)*
- What would the phrase "in the box" suggest? *(If thinking "out of the box" is thinking in a creative way, then "in the box" would suggest thinking the way society has always thought—maintaining the status quo.)*
- The artist's colors are a means of communication. What colors does the artist use and what emotion do the colors evoke? *(The eggs within the box are soft pastel colors, suggesting delicacy. So, the artist evokes a tone of softness, tenderness, and lightness.)*
- How does the artist use vertical and horizontal shapes and lines? *(The artist places the box in the picture vertically. Thus, the egg on the outside is higher than the rest of the eggs. There are somewhat skewed parallel, vertical, and horizontal lines that form the smaller boxes within the larger box. And the canvas has vertical and horizontal lines that form another box that incorporates all of the boxes. The lines are not precisely parallel except for the outside walls of the box. The inside dividers have apparently had to bend or move somewhat to accommodate the various eggs, perhaps indicating that our boundaries/separations change somewhat to meet our needs. The skewed quality of the dividers and somewhat haphazard distribution of the straw-like filling provide a somewhat whimsical quality. The empty space in the box appears to be exactly the size of the white egg.)*

Purpose Questions

Readers must determine the purpose (to inform, entertain, persuade, or explain) of the text if they are to understand it. Determining the purpose of the text provides students with road markers they might otherwise miss, such as bias. Purpose questions for *Out of the Box* might include the following:

- What is Tolliver's purpose in painting this? Is she trying to inform, entertain, or persuade? How do you know? *(Tolliver is attempting to inform her viewer as to the advantages and disadvantages of being in the box.)*

Inference Questions

Students need questions that require them to understand how the parts of the text contribute to the whole text. Each idea or key detail can be re-examined, and through reflective thinking, the student can determine how the idea or detail contributes to the message of the whole text. Inference questions for *Out of the Box* might include the following:

- How does Tolliver convey her argument that there are advantages to being outside of the box? *(The outside egg is bigger, lighter, and brighter than the others, which are of similar size, shape, level of brightness, and somewhat subdued color.)*
- How does Tolliver use symbols, lines, and colors to build the case for the limitations that exist when one is inside the box? How does Tolliver use symbols, lines, and colors to build the case that inside the box offers security? *(The dividers in the box are not straight but instead flex one way or another to provide either limited or expanded room for each egg, depending on the line the divider follows in the box. The colors of the box and the straw-like material are soft and warm, suggesting almost a cozy, homelike quality. The straw material swirls around to make oval nests for the eggs and curves comfortably around their tops.)*
- What do eggs symbolize? How does this symbol contribute to the meaning of the text? *(Eggs are traditionally a symbol of new birth—life, ideas, concepts, movements, resurrection—that can offer positive change. So, the eggs extend the message of possibilities, whereas candy bars inside a box would not offer as many possibilities.)*
- What does blue symbolize and how does the blue impact the message of the painting? *(The color outside the box is blue. Blue is the color of the water and the sea—spaces of vastness and uncharted areas. So, having the blue surrounding the egg outside the box and touching the egg outside the box only expands the opportunities presented to the egg outside the box.)*

Opinion, Argument, and Intertextual Connection Questions

According to Fisher and Frey, the final level of questions should be used sparingly. We are not sure we agree with their assessment, as such questions evoke critical thinking and often result in engaging conversations. There is no doubt that students need to have reread the text numerous times if they are to respond to opinion, argument, and intertextual connection questions. Readers need to have opinions that can be supported with evidence from the text, but we want to encourage students to expand their thinking and argue their perspectives using evidence from other texts. For example, opinion, argument, and intertextual connection questions for *Out of the Box* include the following:

- Does Tolliver make a convincing argument about the advantages of being outside the box? *(Yes, Tolliver makes a convincing argument about the advantages of being outside the box. The egg outside the box is larger; it is not confined by the walls within the box. Yet, there are costs to the freedom. There is no softness; there is only hardness and isolation.)*
- How does Tolliver's box compare with Pandora's box? *(Pandora's box held Envy, Crime, Hate, Disease, and Hope. Pandora released all upon the world. Tolliver's box may well hold a variety of emotions and ideas, but her box contains an empty spot that suggests that perhaps one has escaped and will exist outside the box. Yet, note the egg outside the box is touching the box. So, perhaps the egg is still connected to the box and not completely alone.)*
- Are there other boxes in your world or in history that have or hold significance? If so, can they provide further insight into the meaning of *Out of the Box*? *(My L-shaped desk and the wall next to me form a cubicle of sorts, but the "walls" are only on three sides, so I always have an escape route, unlike the eggs in the box in the painting. Their only option is up, but they lack that capability. In history, the boxes that first occurred to me are the small solitary confinement cells in some prisons. In contrast with my desk "box" and the box in the picture, there is no way out unless someone opens a door. My thoughts turn immediately to how frightening and threatening such a cell must be.)*
- What might Tolliver be suggesting by having a box with no lid? *(There is a way to escape the box; one can leave the cozy soft bed of straw if she/he/it is willing to transcend the walls of the box.)*
- If "in the box" is analogous with society's current assumptions or a reality shared by a community, then "the box" is a metaphor for a paradigm or theoretical framework of a society. So, when one is "outside the box," the accepted pattern or model is broken or transcended. Can you think of a time when a paradigm has been transcended due to thinking outside the box? *(I am thinking of smallpox inoculation. The concept went outside the box, but eventually infiltrated community practices.)*

The Common Core: Reading the Word and Reading the World

Visual literacy is incorporated in College and Career Readiness Anchor Standard 7 for Reading: **Integrate and evaluate content presented in diverse media and formats, including visually and quantitatively, as well as in words.** Before exploring the concept of immigration, a crucial topic of citizenship, it is important to tease out Standard 7 and identify its value in a technological era.

Standard 7 recognizes the twenty-first-century world of students. The reading of visual texts has been recognized as a needed literacy for decades. Yet, too often it has been shortchanged in the classroom, due to the vast amount of content teachers feel pressured to cover. Consequently, some students have acquired the skills needed to perform this process, and others have lacked the consistent exposure needed to build them to proficiency. Too many of our students are novices in their ability to evaluate the content they are bombarded with daily.

Close and critical reading is essential, but, if one does not evaluate the content, then he is vulnerable to distorted truth and/or scams. A 2010 study by the Kaiser Family Foundation revealed children and teens, ages 8 to 18 years of age, on average spend seven hours and thirty-eight minutes a day on some type of media. Often, the students are multitasking (Kaiser 1). Consequently, students are on more than one media at a time during the seven hours and 38 minutes a day. When tallied, not counting multitasking, it means students spend more than 53 hours a week on technology. Now, no one would argue that the ability to evaluate content in diverse media is a critical component of education. Yet, we would argue that it is an essential component of living in the world. Standard 7 is not only a literacy standard, it is a survival standard.

Scams run rampart on the Internet. Often vulnerable victims suffer significant financial loss or worse. If you have email or Facebook, there is a good chance you have been exposed to an urban legend. Evaluating content presented in various media formats is second nature to many teachers. However, teachers spend their lives immersed in literacy. Standard 7 recognizes the fact that American students spend their lives surrounded by literacy, and they must be able to evaluate the content they are exposed to on a daily basis.

Each teacher will know best where to integrate this component of Standard 7 into her curriculum. We recognize that websites are constantly changing; however, we recommend the websites below as sources of reliable information where one can currently fact-check information. Other sites will emerge; it is apparent the scams and inaccuracies in diverse media will only multiply exponentially.

- Snopes ("Rumor Has It.") Do a search for "Snopes" or "urban legends," and this usually comes up as one of the first sites.
- Purportal ("The bunk stops here.") Do a search for "purportal."
- Hoax-slayer ("Debunking email hoaxes and exposing Internet scams since 2003.") Do a search for "hoax-slayer."

It is well worth our time to weave this component of Standard 7 into the curriculum, for it is life literacy in this day and age. The goal is to create close and critical readers who resist blindly accepting as truth what they read on the printed page or screen. They must question, check facts, and evaluate the validity of the texts they read before they incorporate the knowledge into the schema.

SIDENOTE—Cynthia: One of my favorite Facebook postings is the following quote attributed to Abraham Lincoln: "You shouldn't always trust quotes on the Internet!" Granted, the posting is satirical, but I may have to put it on a wall in my classroom to remind my students to evaluate the source of their content. I do not want my students to be passive learners. I do not want to create twenty-first-century citizens who are easily manipulated.

Website Evaluation

The next natural step of implementing Standard 7 is to apply the process of evaluation to websites beyond social media. Rubrics for evaluating websites are not new. They are very accessible through a quick Google search. Kathy Schrock's webpage is a nice starting point when searching for these kinds of rubrics. Her link to critical evaluation provides a critical evaluation survey of websites for elementary, middle, and high school students. However, we strongly encourage teachers to view numerous rubrics and determine what is essential in evaluating a website. Students need to be close and critical readers of all texts. Just because students have personal preferences for certain websites does not mean that they cannot apply a critical eye to them and evaluate their perspectives and agenda. It can be very useful to expose students to bogus or false websites—for example, the website warns of the dangers of dihydrogen monoxide—to illustrate the need to be a critical reader. Have students apply a rubric to evaluate the website. If students carefully evaluate the above website, they will discover dihydrogen monoxide is H_2O, or water, and not a hazardous waste product! See Appendix 4b.1 and 4b.2 for sample rubrics to evaluate websites.

SIDENOTE—Cynthia: I have favorite editorialists, but I always attempt to be a resistant reader. I want to think for myself and not have someone do my thinking for me. I want the same for my students. It is a way of reading and once it is incorporated into your daily routine, it is impossible to turn off the dialogue between you and the text.

Reading Standard 7: Literacy in History/Social Studies

The Reading Standards for Literacy in History/Social Studies for grades six through twelve are in grade groupings. They are as follows for Standard 7:

Grades 6–8. Integrate visual information (e.g., in charts, graphs, photographs, videos, or maps) with other information in print and digital texts.

Grades 9–10. Integrate quantitative or technical analysis (e.g., charts, research data) with qualitative analysis in print or digital text.

Grades 11–12. Integrate and evaluate multiple sources of information presented in diverse formats and media (e.g., visually, quantitatively, as well as in words) in order to address a question or solve a problem).

It is important to note the boldfaced words used in each grade grouping (emphasis added). Though the texts change, the process of integration is consistently noted at each grade level. However, the process of evaluation is not mentioned until the eleventh-and-twelfth-grade group. It is the firm belief of the authors that **evaluating** visual information and other digital text must be woven into the curriculum prior to the last two years of high school. Appendix 4c offers an activity for grades six through eight to meet Reading Standard 7 for Literacy in History/Social Studies. Note that the activity includes an evaluating component.

The Reading Standards for Informational Text in grades four through twelve better flesh out the acquisition of Standard 7 than the Reading Standards for Literacy in History/Social Studies. In addition, there is more distinction between the grades and less grouping. Standard 7 of the Reading Standards for Informational Text in grades four through twelve is as follows:

Reading Standard 7: Informational Text

Grade 4. Interpret information presented visually, orally, or quantitatively (e.g., in charts, graphs, diagrams, timelines, animations, or interactive elements on webpages), and explain how the information contributes to an understanding of the text in which it appears.

Grade 5. Draw on information from multiple print or digital sources, demonstrating the ability to locate an answer to a question quickly or to solve a problem efficiently.

Grade 6. Integrate information presented in different media or formats (e.g., visually, quantitatively) as well as in words to develop a coherent understanding of a topic of issue.

Grade 7. Compare and contrast a text to an audio, video, or multimedia version of the text, analyzing each medium's portrayal of the subject (e.g., how the delivery of a speech affects the impact of the words).

Grade 8. Evaluate the advantages and disadvantages of using different mediums (e.g., print or digital text, video, multimedia) to present a particular topic or idea.

Grades 9–10. Analyze various accounts of a subject told in different mediums (e.g., a person's life story in both print and multimedia), determining which details are emphasized in each account.

Grades 11–12. Integrate and evaluate multiple sources of information presented in different media or formats (e.g., visually, quantitatively) as well as in words in order to address a question or solve a problem.

Note the processes incorporated in Reading Standard 7 for Informational Text. There is more of a clearly defined scaffold for students to acquire the process of evaluation. It is strongly recommended that non-ELA teachers also incorporate these standards into their curriculum, as it provides a road map to the final destination of integration and evaluation of multiple sources of information presented in different types of texts in order to address a question or solve a problem.

Teaching College and Career Readiness Anchor Standard 7 for Reading

Standard 7 requires students to build upon the six standards explored in the previous chapters. Without a firm grasp of Standards 1–6, students will find it difficult to become proficient in Standard 7.

Standard 7 also requires students to **integrate and evaluate content presented in diverse media and formats, including visually and quantitatively, as well as in words.**

> **SIDENOTE—Cynthia:** As a child of the sixties, I identify with this standard. My life was inundated with TV and movies; my children's lives were inundated with computers. The ability to read visual texts closely and critically was crucial to our ability to read the world.

Visual texts are an important element of reading the world. Students are bombarded with visual texts; yet, too often, they do not read the texts closely or critically.

The four questions, noted in Chapter One, are applicable to visual texts. The four questions:

- What does it say?
- How does the text say it?
- What does it mean?
- So, what?

The four questions encourage students to look beyond a surface-level reading of the text, visual or written.

Performance Task: Mining the Potential of a Photograph

Students can apply the same four questions to a visual text. In fact, students need to apply these questions to visual texts if they are to be close and critical readers of their visual world. Students of the twenty-first century are visual; they are visual learners. Consequently, Common Core Standard 7 is one that provides students the opportunity to engage in a world to which they are native learners. Standard 7 is one that provides great potential in the construction of performance tasks or assignments students will find engaging.

Step One: Determination of a Theme

Determine the theme to construct a performance task or a lesson and then seek short texts/sources that could be easily connected in the time span allotted. In addition, consider stimuli that will reach multiple senses. As noted previously in this book, the focus is citizenship of the world and America. Immigration involves citizenship. Since America's conception, immigration has been an ongoing debate; it is an issue that will continue to play a role in the twenty-first century. The texts for this performance task were selected for their various perspectives on immigration. The teacher will have to scaffold students to four texts. Tasks could easily be constructed for two texts or three texts.

Stimuli/Texts: Four texts have been selected for the following performance task.

Performance Task Prompt: Write a constructed response that supports the concept that immigrants have sacrificed to become Americans. Be sure to use evidence from each of the four pieces of text. Note which text best supports the concept of sacrifice and defend your choice with rationale.

Diverse Media and Formats

The four types/genres of text are as follows:

- photograph
- political cartoon
- speech excerpt
- poem

Step Two: Exposure to First Text

Expose students to the first text. In this case, it is a photograph taken at Ellis Island. Ask students to read the photograph, applying the four questions of close and critical reading.

Directions: View the photograph critically. Then answer the following questions.

- What does the text say? (Briefly summarize the photograph at the literal level.)
- How does the photographer say it? In other words, how does the photographer choose to convey his/her purpose? (What are the features, etc.?)
- What does the text mean? (What message/theme/concept is the author trying to get across?)
- So, what? (What does the message/theme/concept mean in your life and/or in the lives of others? Why is it worth sharing/telling? What significance does it have to your life and/or in the lives of others?)

Sample Answers

What does the text say? The picture shows a number of people outside Ellis Island. They appear to be leaving the building. They are carrying suitcases and all have hats on their heads and are wearing coats.

How does the artist say it? The photographer of the black-and-white photograph is unknown. The year is also not provided. However, given the clothes and luggage, one would guess it was taken during the early 1900s. There are many males. Consequently, this picture suggests that more male immigrants landed at Ellis Island than female immigrants. There do not appear to be any families. In addition, there does not appear to be anyone who is elderly, suggesting that immigration was often sought by the young. Furthermore, all the immigrants appear to be white, suggesting that immigration was easier for the white European male. They appear to be carrying or wearing all their possessions. Each has a suitcase and a coat. The photographer used a wide-angle shot (as he/she was able to fit a large group in the shot). Consequently, through the wide shot, the photographer is able to emphasize the subjects in their environment. Also, the wide-angle long shot enables the photographer to show the entire bodies of the subjects. The **point of view** is conveyed through the slightly **high angle of the shot.** In other words, the camera/photographer is looking down upon the subjects. The photographer is in a position of power. This position places the subjects at a lower level than the photographer and conveys a sense of being smaller or less powerful than the photographer. One might assume the photographer is an American, given his/her vantage point. In addition, many of the faces are not turning toward the camera lens, indicating they may not know the picture is being taken. The building is solid, comprised of brick. It represents security but also foreshadows the tests the travelers had to go through before gaining full admittance to America. It is interesting to note the photographer chose to capture such a large band of immigrants. Perhaps he/she is attempting to group the subjects and not distinguish the traits of the mass of people.

What does it mean? Immigrants were primarily white males who started in America with what they could carry. Immigration success was not random but based on tangible traits. This is an example of reciprocity law, which is based on mutual exchange of privileges.

So, what? I am reminded that in this digital age and global world, one does not actually have to immigrate to America to share tangible talents or traits. For example, American corporations can outsource their needs for the financial benefit of all involved. But, perhaps it is only a temporary benefit. The ingenuity and entrepreneurship of the employees remain in their countries of origin whereas the immigrants who come to America bring not only their dreams, but their imagination and courage, traits that will enrich America for generations.

Obviously, the majority of students will not be able to immediately apply these questions to a visual text without plenty of practice. Teachers must scaffold them to independence and proficiency. A good way to scaffold students to this type of close and critical reading of the visual is to:

1) Provide a model of applying the four questions to a photograph.
2) Have the class as a group project apply the four questions to a photograph.
3) Have a small group apply the four questions to a photograph.
4) Have pairs of students apply the four questions to a photograph.
5) Have students individually apply the four questions to a photograph.

In addition, provide students with support tools to complement the instruction. Appendix 4d is a reproducible mine map to support students in their reading of a photograph. The mine maps do not include every possibility; they merely serve as a temporary scaffold for students as they acquire the language of visual literacy; it helps them mine for the ore underneath the surface.

Note that the teacher will need to teach the applicable vocabulary if the mine map is to be a useful tool. There are numerous sites for teachers describing the technical terms and supplying visual examples. There are also PowerPoints on the Reading to the Core website that can be used to teach the type of shots, angles, visual elements, etc. In addition, there are PowerPoint quizzes which teachers can use to check quickly for understanding. Do a search for "Reading to the Core."

SIDENOTE—Cynthia: I have had great success with students acquiring the knowledge by taking assigned shots with their cell phones and sending the shots to me. I then create a PowerPoint of examples with students' photographs, and I credit the photographs to them in the PowerPoint. Even though they are in high school, students take tremendous pleasure in having their photographs exhibited as an example of a long shot, etc.

Close and Critical Reading for a Visual Text

<table>
<tr><th colspan="5">TEXT STRUCTURE: PHOTOGRAPHS</th></tr>
<tr><th>Genre (can blur or cross boundaries)</th><th>Composition</th><th>Point of View</th><th>Tone/Mood</th><th>Visual Elements</th></tr>
<tr>
<td rowspan="2">Photojournalism: Communicate news by photographs, which should be honest and impartial while telling the story. Contribute to news through 1) timeliness, 2) objectivity, 3) narration
Documentary Photography: Fact-based photographs of actual events and people. Can be a form of journalism or social commentary or propaganda or personal expression. Main purpose is to record a place, person(s), or event.
Abstract Photography
Aerial Photography
Architectural Photography
Astrophotography
Fashion Photography
Food Photography
Interior Design Photography
Landscape Photography
Long Exposure Photography
Macro Photography
Pet Photography
Photojournalism
Portrait Photography
Product Photography
Shot Exposure Photography (freezing time)
Sports Photography
Still Life Photography
Street Photography
Time Lapse Video
Underwater Photography
Weather Photography
Wedding Photography
Wildlife Photography</td>
<td rowspan="2">• Rule of thirds: Imagine breaking an image down into thirds (both horizontally and vertically) so that you have nine parts
• Rule of symmetry: Keep your subject symmetrical
• Asymmetry—lack of symmetry or an unevenness to create visual interest
• Background
• Balance—the distribution of the visual elements
• Setting—geographical, temporal, climatic, social
• Subject</td>
<td rowspan="2">• Bird's-eye view
• Angle (POV) includes front, behind, side, top, high, low, eye-level, tilted, neutral, etc.
• Angle—the vantage point
Imagery/ Figures of Speech
• metaphor
• motif
• symbol
• theme
• juxtaposed contrasting concepts
• allusion to previous texts</td>
<td>Capture or evoke emotion through:
• Lighting
• Colors
• Soft focus
• Filters
• Range of tone (What are the darkest and lightest values?)
• Subject expression</td>
<td>Focus (What appears sharpest in the photograph?)
• Light—are there shadows?
• Lines
• Shapes
• Repetition
• Space
• Texture</td>
</tr>
<tr>
<td colspan="2">Photographer's Techniques
• Long Shot (LS) or Full Shot (FS)
• Medium Shot (MS)
• Medium Close-up (MCU)
• Close-up (CU)
• Extreme Close-ups (XCUs)
Technical Concepts
• Shot types (long shot, close up, medium shot)
• Shot length
• Camera angles
• Lighting (backlighting)
• Color
• Framing
• Artistic eye and/or technical mastery
• Use of lighting and color
• Color combination
• Balance
• Details (people, objects, activities)
Unique Perspective
• Tell a story—capture history and/or freeze moment for others to witness (photojournalism does this best)
• Capture an iconic moment
• Leave something to the imagination</td>
</tr>
<tr><td colspan="2">Photographer:</td><td colspan="2">Publication:</td><td>Date of Publication:</td></tr>
</table>

Performance Task: Mining the Potential of a Political Cartoon

WHERE BOTH PLATFORMS AGREE.—NO VOTE—NO USE TO EITHER PARTY.

Step Three: Exposure to Second Text

Expose students to the second text. It is a political cartoon from 1880. Ask students to read the political cartoon, applying the four questions of close and critical reading. See page 62 for directions to a full-color version.

Sample Answers

What does the text say? The political cartoon shows two white men on opposite sides of two posts nailing planks to the posts. One of the planks shows the words "Republican Plan" and the other plank shows the words "Democratic Plan." The front of the plank that the reader can see contains the words "Anti-Chinese." Between the planks is a smaller, darker man; he is barricaded by the planks, and his feet cannot touch the ground. His arms are uplifted with fingers outstretched, and his mouth is open. His eyebrows slant down toward his nose in what appears to be a frown, and his tongue hangs out. Below the political cartoon is a caption: "Where Both Platforms Agree—No Vote—No Use to Either Party." There is a blue sky in the background, and the title of the publication is *Puck*. There is a banner above *Puck* with "What fools these mortals be!" The date of the publication is July 14, 1880. It is Volume VIL – No. 175. The cost is 10 cents.

How does the artist say it? The cartoonist uses **words** to expand his message. Though the picture is of a Chinese man being squeezed in a vice, the words note the two parties (Republicans and Democrats) to clarify who is squeezing the Chinese man. In addition, the **caption** below the cartoon puts in words the message of his cartoon. The artist also uses **caricature** to provide a parody of the two parties. The two men are James Garfield, Republican, and Winfield S. Hancock, Democrat. It is obvious that this is the cover of a newspaper or journal. It notes the **year,** 1880; the **date**, July 14; the **city of publication**, New York; the publisher, Keppler and Schwarzmann; and the title, *Puck*. It also notes the cartoonist in the left corner of the picture, J.A. Wales. The cartoonist makes effective **use of color**. The white men wear white shirts, **contrasting** with the Chinese man, who is significantly darker and is wearing a black shirt to emphasize his darkness. It is also of note that the white men have on very similar clothes (almost a uniform of conformity), emphasizing the difference of the Chinese man caught between them. The planks look as if they may have been pulled from the floor/foundation, as there are two missing ones in the forefront of the picture. There are no women in this cartoon; their opinion of the subject is notably lacking, but then they did not have the right to vote at that time. Finally, the artist relies on **stereotypic images** with the Chinese queue and the platform shoes. The Chinese man's **facial expression** is one of anguish, and his **body expression** conveys a sense of torture. In addition, the artist emphasizes the ancient stereotype of racism; the Chinese man's open mouth and facial expression suggest an animal caught in a trap. One is reminded of the stocks of old, perhaps a **historical allusion**. The **geographical setting** is difficult to determine other than it takes place in America, as is evidenced by the names of the two political parties. Given the clothes and the date of the magazine, one can assume the **temporal setting** of the 1800s.

What does it mean? At the time, immigrants who did not benefit either political party would not be given full citizenship and, consequently, they would not acquire the right to vote and have their voices heard. It is apparent that both parties agreed on the need to limit Chinese immigration.

So, what? I am reminded of the Guest Worker Program. America wants cheap labor but often exploits the laborers from other countries. Furthermore, by denying cheap labor access to citizenship, America ensures that the status quo will be maintained. The Chinese who came to America to build the Transcontinental Railroad were paid less than their white counterparts; they worked longer hours for less pay. However, they could not vote, nor could they testify in court. They were literally silenced. Yet, they endured; such was their desire to become part of America's fabric. America is a patchwork quilt; we are a nation of immigrants who have sacrificed to become part of this great nation.

In 1876, both major political parties included Chinese exclusion in their campaign platforms; in 1882, Congress passed the Chinese Exclusion Act.

Performance Task: Mining the Potential of a Poem

Step Four: Exposure to Third Text

Expose students to the poem "The New Colossus" by Emma Lazarus. Ask students to read the text and apply the four questions of close and critical reading to it. GHR can be a useful strategy to scaffold students to close and critical reading, especially if it is a genre in which they have not had a lot of practice to develop proficiency. Appendix 4f provides GHR prompts for the poem "The New Colossus."

"The New Colossus" by Emma Lazarus

1. Not like the brazen giant of Greek fame
2. With conquering limbs astride from land to land;
3. Here at our sea-washed, sunset gates shall stand
4. A mighty woman with a torch, whose flame
5. Is the imprisoned lightning, and her name
6. Mother of Exiles. From her beacon-hand
7. Glows world-wide welcome; her mild eyes command
8. The air-bridged harbor that twin cities frame.
9. "Keep, ancient lands, your storied pomp!" cries she
10. With silent lips. "Give me your tired, your poor,
11. Your huddled masses yearning to breathe free,
12. The wretched refuse of your teeming shore.
13. Send these, the homeless, tempest-tossed to me,
14. I lift my lamp beside the golden door!"

Sample Answers

What does the text say? This poem states that the new colossus, the "Mother of Exiles," is not like the Greek colossus of old. The new colossus wants the homeless masses desiring to be free. The new colossus, a mighty woman, lifts a lantern to guide the people to her door.

How does the author/poet say it? This **nontraditional sonnet (end of lines rhyme—abbaabbacdcdcd)** is organized by **comparison/contrast** and **description**. The author starts with a historical reference/allusion to the Greek "brazen giant" and contrasts it with the imagery of "a mighty woman." The author's **word choice** of "gates" and "golden door" emphasizes a barrier or entrance at the end of a journey. The author **personifies** the colossus by naming it "Mother of Exiles." In addition, the author uses the **literary device of alliteration**, "world-wide welcome" and "tempest-tossed." The author uses the word "pomp" to **contrast** with the "wretched refuse." The author's reference to a variety of lights ("sunset," "beacon," "golden," etc.) suggests a **motif or recurring idea** of hope. The poem is written from the colossus' **point of view**, and the specific names of the countries and unwanted are noticeably **absent**. The author uses quotation marks to note the statue's words. The author uses **repetition** to emphasize the promise for all: "Give me your…."

What does the text mean? This poem presents America as a land of opportunity for the immigrant. The old world of Europe promised only further economic hardship. However, the new colossus, the Statue of Liberty, promised hope for a new start and a "golden" future. The statue was the gateway to a new life of opportunity. **America awaits the unwanted of Europe.**

So, what? I am struck by who is not noted in the poem. If America is the "Mother of Exiles," then she would love all her children equally. One does not favor one child over another. A mother would want all her children to have equal opportunities.

Performance Task: Mining the Potential of a Speech

Step Five: Exposure to Fourth Text

Directions: Read the excerpt closely and critically. Then answer the four questions of close and critical reading.

President Obama: Remarks on Immigration

Think about it. We define ourselves as a nation of immigrants. That's who we are, in our bones. The promise we see in those who come here from every corner of the globe, that's always been one of our greatest strengths. It keeps our workforce young, it keeps our country on the cutting edge, and it's helped build the greatest economic engine the world has ever known.

After all, immigrants helped start businesses like Google and Yahoo. They created entire new industries that in turn created new jobs and new prosperity for our citizens.

In recent years one in four high-tech startups in America were founded by immigrants. One in four new small-business owners were immigrants; including right here in Nevada, folks who came here seeking opportunity and now want to share that opportunity with other Americans.

But we all know that today we have an immigration system that's out of date and badly broken; a system that's holding us back instead of helping us grow our economy and strengthen our middle class.

Right now we have 11 million undocumented immigrants in America, 11 million men and women from all over the world who live their lives in the shadows. Yes, they broke the rules. They crossed the border illegally. Maybe they overstayed their visas. Those are the facts. Nobody disputes them.

But these 11 million men and women are now here. Many of them have been here for years. And the overwhelming majority of these individuals aren't looking for any trouble. They're contributing members of the community. They're looking out for their families. They're looking out for their neighbors. They're woven into the fabric of our lives.

Every day, like the rest of us, they go out and try to earn a living. Often they do that in the shadow economy, a place where employers may offer them less than the minimum wage or make them work overtime without extra pay. And when that happens, it's not just bad for them, it's bad for the entire economy, because all the businesses that are trying to do the right thing, that are hiring people legally, paying a decent wage, following the rules—they're the ones who suffer.

They've got to compete against companies that are breaking the rules. And the wages and working conditions of American workers are threatened too.

So if we're truly committed to strengthening our middle class and providing more ladders of opportunity to those who are willing to work hard to make it in the middle class, we've got to fix the system....

Sample Answers

What does the text say? America defines herself as a nation of immigrants. Immigrants have been the strength of America, which has benefited from their creativity and economic contributions. Immigrants created Yahoo and Google, among other businesses and industries. Consequently, they have enriched America through jobs and monies. In fact, one in four small businesses and one in four high-tech startups were founded by immigrants. However, immigrants must hide in the shadows because the system of immigration is broken. Consequently, they work for lower wages and are employed by companies that extort their situation. This hurts the American middle class and the companies that play by the rules. The system must be fixed.

How does the speaker say it? The speaker is President Obama, and the **genre** is speech. The setting for the presentation of the speech is Las Vegas, Nevada, which has many immigrants who could identify with the **topic or subject or message** of immigration reform. The speaker uses **first-person plural:** "We define ourselves as a nation of immigrants." Thus, the speaker is identifying with the audience and consequently establishes rapport with his audience. The speaker gives **specific examples** to prove his point that immigrants have helped to create America's economic engine: "...immigrants helped start businesses like Google and Yahoo." The speaker uses a **motif** of the American Dream through his **word choice**, e.g., "promise," "prosperity," and "seeking opportunity." The speaker also uses **statistics** to support his message: "one in four high-tech startups in America were founded by immigrants." The speaker also uses **vernacular language** to create closeness with the audience: "folks who came here seeking opportunity..." The speaker uses **metaphors**: "They're woven into the fabric of our lives." The speaker also uses **imagery**: "men and women from all over the world who live their lives in the shadows."

What does the text mean? America is a nation of immigrants, and if she is to continue to be competitive, then immigration reform needs to be addressed.

So, what? I am reminded of the disease of hemophilia. It was once called the "royal disease." It is an X-linked recessive disorder. It appeared in the royals due to the practice of royalty marrying royalty. So, eventually the kings and queens of Europe were all carriers of the recessive gene. Immigrants are a key to our nation's success. They provide us with fresh blood, ideas, and culture. It is the reason colleges prefer to hire professors who are not graduates of their university or even graduates within their state. To keep ideas generative, it is necessary to feed academia continually with new blood so new knowledge can be constructed.

Step Six: Review Texts

Four texts have been selected for the following performance task: Write a constructed response that supports the concept that immigrants have sacrificed to become Americans. Be sure to use evidence from each of the four pieces of text. Note which text best supports the concept of sacrifice and defend your choice with rationale.

Students' answers will vary greatly, but the teacher determines the criteria and provides the students with a rubric that delineates the skills being assessed.

Teacher Effectiveness and Student Achievement

The recent pressure to show student growth cannot be overstated. We have found that students are not proficient in reading of visual texts, as it has not been a focus in a majority of courses. Consequently, training for students to apply the four questions to a visual text can be an effective way to show student growth. Appendix 4e provides a simple rubric the teacher can use with students who are applying the four questions to a visual text or any text. Previously in the text, we have aligned CCSS to the four questions. We recommend providing students a visual text as a pre-test—for example, a political cartoon at the start of the year. Have students apply the four questions and score their responses with the simple rubric. At the end of the year, provide the same visual text as a post-test. You will be amazed at the student growth.

Chapter Four Works Cited

Kaiser, Henry. Family Foundation. "Generation M2: Media in the Lives of 8-to 18-Year-Olds." Newsroom. 20 January 2010. Web. 9 July 2013.

Keppler, J. "Welcome to all!" Illustration. *Puck* 28 April 1880. Prints and Photographs Online Catalog. American Memory. Lib. of Congress. n.d. Web. 9 July 2013.

Lazarus, Emma. "The New Colossus." *Favorite Poems Old and New.* Ed. Helen Ferris. New York: Doubleday, 1957.

Obama, Barack. "Remarks by the President on Comprehensive Immigration Reform." Del Sol High School, Las Vegas, NV. 29 January 2013. Web. 9 July 2013.

Tolliver, Mary. *Out of the Box.* 2012. Watercolor on Paper. Battle Creek, MI.

Wales. J. A. "Where both platforms agree—no vote—no use to either party." Illustration. *Puck* 14, July 1880. Prints and Photographs Online Catalog. American Memory. Lib. of Congress. n.d. Web. 9 July 2013.

CHAPTER FIVE: **READING FOR ARGUMENT**

Why Argument?

We wrestled with this question too, especially Gerri, who spent most of her 20-plus teaching years in the high school English classroom teaching persuasive writing using Lucile Vaughan Payne's *The Lively Art of Writing* and finding it an exceptional guide through the mysteries of supporting an opinion. In the last few years, though, argument, rather than persuasion, has become a strong focus for college and career readiness.

As a result, a bothersome question continues to crop up: "How does argument differ from persuasion?" Although Smith, Wilhelm, and Fredricksen "don't think the distinction between argument and persuasion is especially useful" (17), we will address that question, along with the components of argument, and provide activities and explanations for CCSS.

When we hear the term argument, mental images begin to form—the fist-pounding political "discussions" that arise around any proposed government policy, the rows over which team is most likely to win the trophy, or even the seemingly universal sibling dispute over who gets to wield the TV remote. *Argument*, here, though, takes a wiser, gentler course that involves logical, reasoned defense of a claim that generally arises from a consideration of data. We will explore forms of argument, terminology associated with argument, and activities to provide students experience with argument. Although writing is an important part of learning about argument, our focus will be on understanding argument texts.

Forms of Argument

Fact, Judgment, and Policy

Aristotle's three forms of argument—forensic, epideictic, and deliberative—appear in George Hillocks Jr.'s *Teaching Argument Writing: Grades 6–12* as fact, judgment, and policy.

Storyteller's View: Global Heroes

Our focus on global citizenship brought us to the work of global leaders, where we found material that stretched our thinking and we hope it will challenge others as well.

Orphans International Worldwide has the motto "Raising Global Citizens." This group identified 36 global heroes to provide children with models. These champions are strong reminders of the heady possibilities inherent in following a role model.

Winston Churchill, one of our favorites on the list, bridges the gap between argument and persuasion. The unadorned reasoning in his first speech to the House of Commons contains his famous line about what he had to offer in the struggle that lay ahead, but he also outlined what the country might expect. They had a terrible war to fight, but they would unify and survive, no matter how hard it was (Churchill "Blood, Toil, Tears, and Sweat"). In later speeches, at times he moved into more emotional appeal, particularly the last, moving paragraph of his June 4, 1940 speech to the House of Commons in which he provided a sobering update on the war and then listed all the places the British would fight the enemy (Churchill "We Shall Fight on the Beaches").

- **Arguments of fact** involve analyzing and interpreting evidence and using the resulting ideas and information to provide support for a factual claim. Hillocks Jr. uses "Whodunit?" mysteries as beginning points for teaching students about arguments of fact (Hillocks Jr. 15–6). A claim in an argument of fact might be:
  - o *The butler did it.*
  - o *The economy is recovering.*
  - o *Eating a Mediterranean diet is the best approach to good health.*

We use logically presented reasoning and factual information to defend an argument of fact.

- **Arguments of judgment** involve such strategies as choosing criteria, selecting attributes, and identifying reasons to expand a definition of a key concept (Hillocks Jr. 41–2), including freedom, wisdom, honor, or love. A claim in an argument of judgment might be:
  - o *The politician is a* ***wise*** *man.*
  - o *The war was* ***justifiable****.*
  - o *Tough love is* ***true love****.*

To defend an argument of judgment, we certainly want logically developed reasoning and factual information, but we often need to develop our defense by clarifying the key judgment involved by thoroughly explaining the definition for the audience. In our examples, we would ask "Just what does being wise, labeling something as **justifiable**, or the idea of **true love** mean?"

- **Arguments of policy** involve determining what is acceptable in a situation, expanding definitions, and even carrying out an investigation to use as evidence in a claim that may address policies, rules, procedures, etc. (Hillocks Jr. 66–7). A claim in an argument of policy might be:
  - o *The school needs an open-lunch policy.*
  - o *America should devote more money to its educational system.*
  - o *Recycling should be a law.*

As we support an argument of policy, we might draw on the strategies used in fact and judgment, but we need to concentrate on defending what makes the rule or policy justifiable.

Activity: Switch Hitting!

Learning to switch a topic from one argument form to another can increase students' understanding of the three forms in text. These examples, based on *The U.S. Constitution* by Jean Kinney Williams, a text outlining basic information on the U.S. Constitution, might result in these argument claims:

- **Factual Argument Claims**
  - o Shays' Rebellion led to the U.S. Constitution.
  - o The issue of selecting representatives slowed the process of developing the U.S. Constitution.
- **Judgment Argument Claims**
  - o The U.S. Constitution was a landmark document for its time.
  - o The U.S. Constitution lays out a perfect union.
- **Policy Argument Claims**
  - o The United States should have three co-presidents, each representing a different part of the country, as Benjamin Franklin suggested.
  - o Amendments to the U.S. Constitution should be submitted to a popular vote.

Activity: Claim Practice

Provide a list of claims of fact, judgment, and policy mixed in with statements of fact, and ask students to identify them. Then ask students to write an example of each type of claim, either by changing the ones you have given them or by developing new ones.

Directions: Identify each statement on the list as one of the following:

A. Statement of Fact
B. Fact Claim
C. Judgment Claim
D. Policy Claim

1. The United States of America has 50 states.
2. The United States of America should add Puerto Rico as its 51st state.
3. The United States of America should adopt Benjamin Franklin's idea of having three presidents. (Supporting this claim requires arguing for a change in our present laws.)
4. Benjamin Franklin was one of the founding fathers of the United States.
5. Benjamin Franklin was the most versatile of the founding fathers.

Answers

1. Statement of Fact (Research proves that the United States of America has 50 states.)
2. Policy Claim (Supporting statehood for Puerto Rico would require providing reasons for a change in present laws/policies.)
3. Policy Claim (Supporting a change to three presidents would require providing reasons for a change in present laws/policies.)
4. Statement of Fact (Historical documents prove that Franklin was a founding father.)
5. Judgment Claim (Supporting this claim would require explanation of what the writer means by *versatile* and then offering reasons why Franklin fits that definition better than any of the founding fathers.)

Added Practice

Now change each of the five statements above into a different form. For example, you might change *The United States of America has 50 states*, a statement of fact, to a judgment claim by revising it to *The United States of America has/has not been overly cautious in keeping the number of states at 50.*

Activity: Claim Identification

Read the following text excerpts and identify the claim(s) in each one.

1. "The Northwest Ordinance gave all newly admitted states the same rights as existing states. The Constitutional Convention delegates wisely let that rule stand. Historians have since agreed that giving new states fewer rights than the first thirteen probably would have inspired more revolution" (Williams 32).

Answer: *The middle sentence about delegates is a judgment claim, as it requires explanation of why the convention delegates were "wise." The first sentence is a statement of fact, and the last sentence provides support for the claim.*

2. "At the same time, the Constitution was broad enough to allow for future growth and change in government. For example, the Constitution granted Congress the power to pass any law considered 'necessary and proper' for it to carry on its duties. More importantly, the Constitution was made the 'supreme law' of the land—all three branches of the federal government, as well as state governments, must stay within its boundaries" (Williams 33).

Answer: *The first sentence states a claim, although it is not an especially controversial one, to serve as a basis for argument. However, the second sentence does provide support for the claim. The third sentence turns somewhat to address the strength of the Constitution, rather than its breadth, but it does provide some additional support.*

Argument vs. Persuasion

One of the most likely questions about argument is "How does persuasion differ from argument?" New teachers as well as experienced teachers who have been addressing persuasion for years are now wondering how those familiar elements and strategies mesh or conflict with the newly increased focus on argument. Although an argument writer may draw occasionally on writing techniques commonly found in persuasive text and the overall goal of both is to convince a reader, the two text forms do differ.

Storyteller's View: A Passion for Persuasion

Sadly, intense persuasion can run amuck. The ineffective writer may rely on soul-baring, "tell-all" prose that can be passionate or even fiery, but may have little substance. A careful reader must separate the quality of the delivery from the intensity of the subject. Isolating the writing from the topic in such situations is not always easy, yet doing so may be critical for the reader to gain accurate understanding.

We see this concern extending to some reality shows that are quickly becoming the standard by which our students judge behavior—and their own view of the world. Unfortunately, that standard may reflect a value system that distorts the importance of some aspects of life. Learning to judge when an argument has its base in logic and evidence will help students as they make critical decisions about the texts they read and view.

The writer of persuasive text has an arsenal of strategies to entice the reader to accept his opinion, selecting the most favorable evidence and then at times drawing on style and sincere appeals to the emotions or beliefs to influence the reader. The persuasive writer may feel strongly that the position supported in the text is the *right* one and may defend his beliefs with considerable intensity. At times, persuasive pieces attempt to persuade as a result of the skill or personality of the writer, rather than as a result of the strength of the defense. Weaker persuasive writers may lose control of an emotional appeal and relate melodramatic scenes designed to tug at the hearts of the audience because they may not have the writing skill to develop a strong persuasive defense.

The argument writer, on the other hand, bases her case on logic and tends to be less likely to involve emotions. The argument's force rests on strong evidence, warrants, backing, qualifiers, and even rebuttals to support the claim. When the argument writer loses control or has little skill, the result tends to be lack of convincing evidence or failure to back up the claim rather than emotional appeals. Both persuasion and argument have places in the skillful writer's repertoire.

Activity: Identification of Pros and Cons and Components in a Sample Argument

The argument writer needs a reasonable level of knowledge about the topic in order to develop a convincing defense of her claims. Let's look at information that might lead to a claim and then explore how a writer might defend that claim.

Paraphrased Background Data

Tobacco kills approximately 443,000 Americans annually, making it the main cause of early and avoidable deaths. The United States pays $96 billion for medical expenses and $97 billion for the loss of worker output every year as a result of cigarette smoking (U.S. Department of Health and Human Services).

Over 400,000 people die in the United States each year as a consequence of smoking cigarettes and being in the vicinity of smoke from the cigarettes of others. These two factors are also primary reasons that people face disability early in their lives (Centers for Disease Control and Prevention).

Sample Argument

Congress should pass a nationwide federal smoking ban in all public places. Although some might argue that the state legislatures should be the bodies to address this issue, the combined Senate and House of Representatives consolidate the law-making power for the entire nation, and trying to accomplish this one state at a time would take too long. Admittedly, this prohibition should not apply to private property, such as an individual's home. A ban that covered private homes would be too extreme. However, smoking has been proven dangerous not only to the smoker, but also to others who encounter the smoke—a problem that is simply too large to ignore. In fact, smoking cigarettes and being in contact with secondhand smoke lead to over 400,000 lost lives yearly in this country. These factors are also major contributors to early disability (Centers for Disease Control and Prevention). The health of innocent citizens definitely outweighs smokers' rights because one person's rights may not prevail over another person's safety. Clearly, the time for this ban has arrived.

Identification of pros and cons. Provide students with a copy of the sample argument above. Divide them into two groups or in pairs. One group or partner identifies the pros, and the other identifies the cons. When they have had sufficient time, have partners compare their work.

Sample argument: pros underlined **and cons** ***italicized.*** Congress should pass a nationwide federal smoking ban in all public places. *Although some might argue that the state legislatures should be the bodies to address this issue,* the combined Senate and House of Representatives consolidate the law-making power for the entire nation, and trying to accomplish this one state at a time would take too long. *Admittedly, this prohibition should not apply to private property such as an individual's home. A ban that covered private homes would be too extreme.* However, smoking has been proven dangerous not only to the smoker, but also to others who encounter the smoke—a problem that is simply too large to ignore. In fact, smoking cigarettes and being in contact with secondhand smoke lead to over 400,000 lost lives yearly in this country. These factors are also major contributors to early disability (Centers for Disease Control and Prevention). The health of innocent citizens definitely outweighs *smokers' rights* because one person's rights may not prevail over another person's safety. Clearly, the time for this ban has arrived.

Activity: Argument Sample Components	
Background Data	Tobacco kills approximately 443,000 Americans annually, making it the main cause of early and avoidable deaths. The United States pays $96 billion for medical expenses and $97 billion for the loss of worker output every year as a result of cigarette smoking (U.S. Department of Health and Human Services). Over 400,000 people die in the United States each year as a consequence of smoking cigarettes and being in the vicinity of smoke from the cigarettes of others. These two factors are also primary reasons that people face disability early in their lives (Centers for Disease Control and Prevention). *The writer examines data that raises questions that eventually lead to a claim. Examining this data, a writer might ask, for example, "What might reduce or even eliminate this problem?" The writer's answer to the question leads to a claim.*
Claim	Congress should pass a nationwide federal smoking ban in all public places. *A claim does just that—asserts something based on evidence that the writer believes to be worthy of recognition or acceptance*
Counter Claim	Although some might argue that the state legislatures should be the bodies to address this issue, *A counter claim brings up a point that an opposing side might raise.*
Rebuttal	the combined Senate and House of Representatives consolidate the law-making power for the entire nation, and trying to accomplish this one state at a time would take too long. *A rebuttal addresses a counter claim that might be raised by someone with an opposing view.*

Activity: Argument Sample Components	
Counter Claim	Admittedly, this prohibition should not apply to private property such as an individual's home. A ban that covered private homes would be too extreme. *Because claims are rarely absolutely true, we may need to limit or modify them, sometimes by simply conceding a point before the opposition raises it.*
Reason	However, smoking has been proven to be dangerous not only to the smoker, but also to others who encounter the smoke—a problem that is simply too large to ignore. *Reasons support the claim. The intent here is to outweigh the private-home argument.*
Evidence	In fact, smoking cigarettes and being in contact with secondhand smoke lead to over 400,000 lost lives yearly in this country. These factors are also major contributors to early disability (Center for Disease Control). *Evidence supports the claim, often by backing up a reason.*
Reason	The health of innocent citizens definitely outweighs smokers' rights because one person's rights may not prevail over another person's safety. *Reasons support claims.*
Concluding Claim	Clearly, the time for this ban has arrived. *A claim states a position that the writer believes should be accepted.*

Argument Component Questions

Now let's take that same argument sample and look at questions the reader might ask to help identify the parts of the argument.

Claim

To find the claim, a reader might ask:

- What position does the writer want me to accept?
- Where does the writer tell me what he or she believes *should* happen? (The word *should* might be a clue, but the writer in our sample could easily have said, "Congress *needs to/must/ought* to pass a national federal smoking ban.")

Counter Claim

To find a counter-claim/argument, a reader might ask:

- Do I read anything that seems to admit or concede a point to the opposing side?
- Do I see anything introduced by a transition, such as *some say, it is true that,* or *admittedly*?

Reasons

To identify a reason, a reader might ask:

- What do I read that provides support for the claim?

Rebuttal

To find a rebuttal, a reader might ask:

- Do I read anything that presents a defense against a counter-claim/argument?

Delineation and Evaluation of Argument: Theodore Roosevelt's Letter Excerpt: Grade 8 Standard

Let's turn to a sample from a presidential text, an excerpt from a letter to American school children from President Theodore Roosevelt. The entire text, though relatively short, is at a higher reading level (approximately eleventh grade), but look for it in Appendix 5a if you would prefer to work with the entire text. Introduce vocabulary words prior to reading the letter to assist younger students in understanding—or do a GHR.

Argument Sample: Grades 6–8 Reading Level

Excerpt from a Proclamation by President Theodore Roosevelt to the School Children of the United States (1907)

"A people without children would face a hopeless future; a country without trees is almost as hopeless; forests which are so used that they can not renew themselves will soon vanish, and with them all their benefits. A true forest is not merely a storehouse full of wood, but, as it were, a factory of wood, and at the same time a reservoir of water. When you help to preserve our forests or to plant new ones you are acting the part of good citizens. The value of forestry deserves, therefore, to be taught in the schools, which aim to make good citizens of you. If your Arbor Day exercises help you to realize what benefits each one of you receives from the forests, and how by your assistance these benefits may continue, they will serve a good end" (Roosevelt 1).

Concluding Paragraph Informal Lexile Level: 1130L

Delineation and Evaluation of Roosevelt's Letter (Grade 8 Standard)

CCSS.ELA-Literacy.RI.8.8: **Delineate and evaluate** the argument and specific claims in a text, assessing whether the reasoning is sound and the evidence is relevant and sufficient; recognize when irrelevant evidence is introduced.

Walk through Roosevelt's paragraph with students, identifying its components, suggesting that they highlight each part in some easily distinguishable way. You may wish to have them highlight or underline in different colors, use pencil and pen, highlight on a computer, or use any other means of identification that works best. Don't worry about fine-tuning the claim-vs.-reason divisions as long as students get the idea that Roosevelt is:

1. claiming that we need to preserve and plant trees and
2. supplying reasons that support his claim.

Claims underlined and reasons *italicized*. A people without children would face a hopeless future; a country without trees is almost as hopeless; *forests which are so used that they can not renew themselves will soon vanish, and with them all their benefits. A true forest is not merely a storehouse full of wood, but, as it were, a factory of wood, and at the same time a reservoir of water. When you help to preserve our forests or to plant new ones you are acting the part of good citizens.* The value of forestry deserves, therefore, to be taught in the schools, *which aim to make* *good citizens of you. If your Arbor Day exercises help you to realize what benefits each one of you receives from the forests, and how by your assistance these benefits may continue,* they will serve a good end.

Talk through the paragraph with students, asking for comments on *how* Roosevelt's argument develops in this concluding section. If students recognize the metaphors, that's wonderful, but those elements of author's craft are not essential to this discussion. Remind them that we are examining the *effectiveness* of the argument. When you are confident that students understand how effectively the argument develops, ask them to write an analysis of the paragraph that discusses how the argument develops and *how effective* it is. You may want to refer to the following sample answer for ideas to draw into your discussion questions.

Sample Answer—How Effectively Does Theodore Roosevelt Develop His Argument?
This paragraph concludes President Roosevelt's letter to American school children by refocusing on what he would like them to do and why. He emphasizes the importance of America's forests in his ***claim*** *(trees are vital to America's future) by providing* ***reasons*** *that contain a somewhat indirect, yet undeniably clear, comparison when he says that a future without trees would be almost as hopeless as a future without children. Then he develops his* ***reasons*** *using three highly effective and rather original metaphors when he compares a forest to a storehouse, a factory, and a reservoir, for trees store and create wood and hold water. He continues to present* ***reasons*** *with his comment on being "good citizens" in planting and preserving trees, extending this to another* ***reason*** *by his* ***claim*** *that forestry "deserves to be taught" in the schools—again reinforcing the concept of the students becoming "good citizens." He ends the paragraph and the letter with another clear focus on his* ***claim*** *by suggesting that if Arbor Day activities help students to understand and appreciate the importance of forests and students' role in protecting them, "they will serve a good end."*

Argument in Visual Text

We would be remiss if we ignored the potential for argument in visual text, one of the most persuasive ways to present and/or support a claim, if done well. (See Chapter 4 for deeper coverage of visual text.) In the first political cartoon to appear in America, the "Join, or Die" cartoon from the Library of Congress American Memory site, the colonies appear as separate segments of a serpent with an arrow tongue.

Visual Argument Activity 1: "Join, or Die" Political Cartoon

Pair students and provide them with a copy of the cartoon and a set of questions such as the following. (See Chapter 4 for additional suggestions for visual text activities.)

- What might Franklin have been suggesting about the direction of his serpent? Support your answer with references to the text. *(Things to consider: the serpent has a single arrow for a tongue, and it points ahead in a fairly straight direction, although somewhat downward focused. A more common serpent tongue would be forked, suggesting two directions.)*
- Is Franklin's claim that the colonists' only choices were to join or die reasonable and well supported? *(The answer may at first seem obvious, particularly since the creator carries the status of a founding father, yet digging just a bit deeper may raise a doubt: Are the only alternatives to join or to die? Certainly the colonists may have been risking death, yet was death a single definite alternative?)*

Visual Argument Activity 2: "Election Day!" Political Cartoon

Provide students with a copy of the women's suffrage cartoon from the Library of Congress American Memory site and the following writing prompt.

What claim is the cartoonist making about women's suffrage? Support your answer with details from the cartoon. Be sure that the claim is supported by relevant and sufficient evidence from the cartoon.

Sample answer: The cartoonist seems to be suggesting that extending the vote to women will change traditional roles, most likely in negative ways. Support for this claim:

- *The man, presumably the father, is holding the babies.*
- *The woman has a somewhat masculine-looking coat, whereas the man has a lengthy, somewhat feminine-looking apron.*
- *"Votes for Women" is prominent on a sign on the wall.*
- *Both babies are crying, yet the woman appears to be preparing to leave.*
- *The expression on the man's face suggests surprise (raised eyebrows) and sadness or possibly even despair (creased brow). His mouth is open—perhaps in a plea?*
- *The expression on the woman's face seems to display no emotion (no curvature to the lips except a downward tilt at the edges, appearing quite set, almost disapproving).*
- *The tea kettle is steaming, adding to the pressure of the situation.*
- *A flier for the "Hen Party" lies at the bottom of the picture.*
- *The cat's arched back and wide-eyed expression seem to suggest surprise.*
- *The wash hung on the clothesline suggests housework to be done.*
- *The broken plate on the floor may be an indication that things are not going well in the household.*

Argument Terminology

The Common Core Informational Reading Standard 8, reading for argument, has drawn considerable attention to argument. Terms of argument, as set forth in the standards, appear in the charts below, along with argument terms as presented in Toulmin and Hillocks Jr.

Common Core Informational Reading Standard 8 Grade Introduced	
Terms • Reasons (4) • Evidence (4) • Points (4) • Claims (6) • Argument (6) • Relevant evidence (7) • Irrelevant evidence (8) • False statements (9) • Fallacious reasoning (9) • Seminal U.S. texts (11) • Premises (11) • Purposes (11) • Public advocacy (11) • Constitutional principles (11) • Legal reasoning (11)	**Processes** • Explain (4) • Support (4) • Trace (6) • Evaluate (6) • Distinguish (6) • Assess (7) • Delineate (8) • Evaluate (8)

Added Terms	
Hillocks Jr. • Evidence • Data • Warrant • Backing • Qualification • Counter Argument • Argument of Fact • Argument of Judgment • Argument of Policy	**Toulmin** • Claim • Evidence • Warrant • Backing • Qualification • Rebuttal

We have practiced exploring some of these terms in sample texts. As an aid for teachers, we have also included the Common Core Reading Informational Text standards addressing argument (8), with boldfaced, grade-by-grade skill development. Additional material in Appendix 5b addresses argument as presented through the grades using a sample argument claim on pizza for lunch in a school.

Pull the key skills out of the standards for a pre-test and post-test. It's often helpful to focus on the key verbs when developing activities for the assessments, particularly when the standard contains more than one. For example, "trace and evaluate" calls for two separate skills. Find the key skills in the standards listed here, or look on the chart on page 99.

Standard 8: Grade-by-grade Skill Development

English Language Arts Informational Text Standards

CCSS.ELA–Literacy.RI.4.8: Explain how an author uses reasons and evidence to support particular points in a text.

CCSS.ELA–Literacy.RI.5.8: Explain how an author uses reasons and evidence to support particular points in a text, **identifying which reasons and evidence support which point(s).**

CCSS.ELA-Literacy.RI.6.8: **Trace and evaluate the argument and specific claims** in a text, **distinguishing claims that are supported by reasons and evidence from claims that are not.**

CCSS.ELA–Literacy.RI.7.8: Trace and evaluate the argument and specific claims in a text, **assessing whether the reasoning is sound and the evidence is relevant and sufficient to support the claims.**

CCSS.ELA–Literacy.RI.8.8: **Delineate and evaluate** the argument and specific claims in a text, assessing whether the reasoning is sound and the evidence is relevant and sufficient; **recognize when irrelevant evidence is introduced.**

CCSS.ELA–Literacy.RI.9–10.8: Delineate and evaluate the argument and specific claims in a text, assessing whether the reasoning is valid and the evidence is relevant and sufficient; **identify false statements and fallacious reasoning.**

CCSS.ELA–Literacy.RI.11–12.8: Delineate and evaluate the reasoning **in seminal U.S. texts, including the application of constitutional principles and use of legal reasoning (e.g., in U.S. Supreme Court majority opinions and dissents) and the premises, purposes, and arguments in works of public advocacy (e.g., *The Federalist*, presidential addresses).**

History/Social Studies Literacy Standards

CCSS.ELA–Literacy.RH.6–8.8: Distinguish among fact, opinion, and reasoned judgment in a text.

CCSS.ELA–Literacy.RH.9–10.8: Assess the extent to which the reasoning and evidence in a text support the author's claims.

CCSS.ELA–Literacy.RH.11–12.8: Evaluate an author's premises, claims, and evidence by corroborating or challenging them with other information.

Sample Pre-test/Post-test: Argument—Grades 9 and 10

Grade-by-grade Skill Chart: Standard 8

Grade	Skill	Skill	Skill
6.8	Trace & evaluate • the argument and • specific claims.	Distinguish • claims supported by reasons and evidence. • claims that are not supported by reasons and evidence.	
7.8	Trace & evaluate • the argument and • specific claims.	Assess whether • reasoning is sound and • evidence is • relevant and • sufficient.	
8.8	Delineate & evaluate • the argument and • specific claims.	Assess whether • reasoning is sound and • evidence is • relevant and • sufficient.	Recognize when irrelevant evidence is introduced.
9.8 & 10.8	Delineate & evaluate • the argument and • specific claims.	Assess whether • reasoning is sound and • evidence is • relevant and • sufficient.	Identify • false statements and • fallacious reasoning.
11.8 & 12.8	Delineate and evaluate reasoning **in seminal U.S. texts:** • application of constitutional principles, • use of legal reasoning (e.g., in U.S. Supreme Court majority opinions and dissents), and • works of public advocacy (e.g., ***The Federalist,*** presidential addresses), including • premises, • purposes, and • arguments.		

We have included a sample assessment for students in grades 9 and 10, based on the sample argument text that begins on page 101 (and repeated with answers on page 102). The two main tasks are "Reading and Identification Task" and "Evaluation Writing Prompt."

Reading and Identification Task

Read the argument sample and identify as many of the following elements as you can, either highlighting them on your copy, circling or underlining, or listing them on another paper (more time consuming). When you are satisfied that you have identified all the key components, write a response to the prompt below.

- Main Claim or Argument
- Claim
- Insufficiently Supported Claim
- Counterargument
- Rebuttal
- Relevant Evidence
- Irrelevant Evidence
- False Statement
- Fallacious/Unsound Reasoning

Evaluation Writing Prompt

Write an evaluation of the sample argument in which you do the following:

- Explain the structure of the argument, remembering to include specific claims.
- Evaluate the argument section by section, being sure to include comments on whether or not the reasoning/thinking is sound.
- For each claim, include a discussion of whether or not the evidence is
  - o relevant and
  - o sufficient to support the claim.
- Identify any false statements and fallacious or misleading reasoning you find.

Argument Background Information

Paraphrased Data

Scores for seniors in high school went down from 2006 to 2010, with fewer students scoring at or above Proficient in 2010 (Center for History and New Media 1).

Levine's research revealed that, when considered in any "reasonable way," the percentage of youths getting involved has gone down since 1972 (Levine 5).

A review of what young people in the United States learn about being responsible citizens reveals deficits. Surveys of teens' opinions demonstrate a lack of commitment to volunteering in the community (Dirksen 1).

At the local level, governments are involving young people by seeking youth representation on advisory boards and commissions, allotting spots for youth members on city councils, and creating youth commissions or boards to provide governing groups advice on topics concerning young people (Municipal Research and Services Center 1).

Sample Argument Text—Student Version

Today's young people have access to more information about the world around them than ever before in history. With the click of a mouse or the flick of a finger on a touch screen, every young person has the ability to read incredibly detailed reports covering the activities of just about any local, state, or national governmental body. Despite this access, far too many of our youths live in an unknowing fog that tends never to clear enough to provide a distinct view of the world around them. One possible remedy for this sad state is to make active attendance at state, local, or national government meetings a graduation requirement.

Admittedly, some will argue that the schools have the responsibility to teach civic awareness and encourage such involvement—or that parents should model such participation. However, these approaches have not succeeded. A research compilation by Levine and Lopez revealed that youth percentages reflecting youth involvement have gone down since 1972 (Levine 5). Another factor that complicates, and possibly even causes, this lack of involvement is a knowledge deficit that seems to be growing, as the National Assessment of Educational Progress reveals that seniors' civics scores were lower in 2010 than they were in 2006, with a lower percentage scoring Proficient or above in 2010 (Center for History and New Media 1). If the present system were working, young people would be more involved in governmental activities, even just local commissions, and they would know more about the actions and guidelines of such groups. A knowledgeable young person might opt for inclusion in rather than exclusion from "the system" if that same system had proven its usefulness and importance. Regrettably, it has not.

What, then, would be a plausible solution to this problem? A Municipal Research and Services Center examination of the methods various groups were using to draw in young people and thus increase their awareness of government operations revealed that local governing bodies such as boards and councils are involving young people by creating youth member or youth representative spots and establishing youth advisory groups (Municipal Research and Services Center of Washington 1). Such programs are worthy of commendation, yet although an invitational program might draw a number of students into the public arena as observers or possibly even active participants, anyone working with youth will attest that invitations won't work for teens, even those who are already the most actively involved. A graduation requirement would place a much-needed incentive into the student's decision-making: the desire to march to the podium at graduation and have Mom and Dad witness the receipt of a signed, sealed diploma from a school official.

Clearly, active involvement, at least to the level of attendance, would very likely help to fill the civics knowledge gap as well as encourage continued participation. The fear factor of reluctance to face a somewhat threatening new situation would be overcome by the simple measure of making attendance a school function that has the security and comfort-producing advantages of being something everyone must do. A few years later, after graduation, and when an issue of concern arises, every one of these students will be attending a city commission meeting, a state opinion-gathering forum, or even a national political candidate's speech. Won't that be its own reward?

Sample Argument Text—Identified Components

Today's young people have access to more information about the world around them than ever before in history. With the click of a mouse or the flick of a finger on a touch screen, **[False Statement]** every young person has the ability to read incredibly detailed reports covering the activities of just about any local, state, or national governmental body. Despite this access, far too many of our youths live in an unknowing fog that tends never to clear enough to provide a distinct view of the world around them. **[Central Argument/Claim]** One possible remedy for this sad state is to make active attendance at state, local, or national government meetings a graduation requirement.

[Counterargument 1] Admittedly, some will argue that the schools have the responsibility to teach civic awareness and encourage such involvement—**[Counterargument 2]** or that parents should model such participation. **[Rebuttal]** However, these approaches have not succeeded. **[Evidence 1]** *A research compilation by Levine and Lopez revealed that percentages reflecting youth involvement have gone down since 1972 (Levine 5).* Another factor that complicates, and possibly even causes, this lack of involvement is a knowledge deficit that seems to be growing, as the National Assessment of Educational Progress reveals: **[Evidence 2]** *reveals that seniors' civics scores were lower in 2010 than they were in 2006, with a lower percentage scoring Proficient or above in 2010 (Center for History and New Media 1).* **[Insufficiently Supported Claim]** If the present system were working, young people would be more involved in governmental activities, even just local commissions, and they would know more about the actions and guidelines of such groups. **[Claim]** A knowledgeable young person might opt for inclusion in rather than exclusion from "the system" if that same system had proven its usefulness and importance. **[Unsupported Claim]** Regrettably, it has not.

What, then, would be a plausible solution to this problem? **[Evidence 3]** *A Municipal Research and Services Center examination of the methods various groups were using to draw in young people and thus increase their awareness of government operations revealed that local governing bodies, such as boards and councils, are involving young people by youth member or youth representative spots and establishing youth advisory groups (Municipal Research and Services Center of Washington 1).* Such programs are worthy of commendation, yet **[Counterargument 3]** although an invitational program might draw a number of students into the public arena as observers or possibly even active participants, **[Fallacious Reasoning/False Claim]** anyone working with youth will attest that invitations won't work for teens, even those who are already the most actively involved. **[Claim]** A graduation requirement would place a much-needed incentive into the student's decision-making: the desire to march to the podium at graduation and have Mom and Dad witness the receipt of a signed, sealed diploma from a school official.

[(Concluding) Claim] Clearly, active involvement, at least to the level of attendance, would very likely help to fill the civics knowledge gap as well as encourage continued participation. **[Insufficiently Supported Claim]** The fear factor of reluctance to face a somewhat threatening new situation would be overcome by the simple measure of making attendance a school function that has the security and comfort-producing advantages of being something everyone must do. **[Fallacious Reasoning/False Claim]** A few years later, after graduation, when an issue of concern arises, every one of these students will be attending a city commission meeting, a state opinion-gathering forum, or even a national political candidate's speech. Won't that be its own reward?

Chapter Five Works Cited

Centers for Disease Control and Prevention. "Tips from Former Smokers 2013 Campaign. Atlanta: USA.gov. 1 April 2013. 3 April 2013. http://www.cdc.gov/Features/SmokersTips/index.html

Center for History and New Media. "Study Shows Lack of Civics Knowledge by U.S. Students." National Coalition for History. 6 May 2011. Web. 4 July 2013.

Churchill, Winston. "Blood, Toil, Tears, and Sweat: May 14, 1940, First Speech to House of Commons." *Speeches.* The Churchill Centre. 29 July 2010. Web. 21 October 2013.

- - - - - - - - - - - - . "We Shall Fight on the Beaches: June 4, 1940, House of Commons" *Speeches.* The Churchill Centre. Web. 21 October 2013.

Dirksen Congressional Center. "Citizenship." *Congress for Kids.* n.d. Web. 4 July 2013.

Franklin, Benjamin. "Join or Die." Illustration. *The Pennsylvania Gazette* 9 May 1754. *Prints and Photographs Online Catalog.* 02 Dec. 2005. *American Memory.* Lib. of Congress. 31 Jan. 2006. Web. 9 July 2013.

Gustin, E.W. "Election Day." Illustration. *Votes for Women's Suffrage Pictures, 1850-1920.* Library of Congress. c1909. Web. 9 July 2013.

Hillocks Jr., George. *Teaching Argument Writing, Grades 6-12: Supporting Claims with Relevant Evidence and Clear Reasoning.* Portsmouth, NH: Heinemann, 2011.

"Key Points in English Language Arts." *Common Core State Standards Initiative.* 2012. Web. 9 May 2013.

Levine, Peter, and Mark Hugo Lopez. "Fact Sheet: Youth Voter Turnout Has Declined, by Any Measure." Center for Information and Research on Civic Learning and Engagement. September 2002. Web. 4 July 2013.

Municipal Research and Services Center of Washington. "Youth Participation in Local Government." June 2012. Web. 7 July 2013.

Roosevelt, Theodore. "A Proclamation by President Theodore Roosevelt, 1907: To the School Children of the United States." Arbor Day Foundation. n.d. Web. 5 April 2013.

Smith, Michael W., Jeffrey D. Wilhelm, and James E. Fredricksen. *Oh, Yeah! Putting Argument to Work Both in School and Out.* Portsmouth, NH: Heinemann, 2012.

U.S. Department of Health and Human Services. *Preventing Tobacco Use Among Young People: A Report of the Surgeon General. Executive Summary.* Rockville, MD: 2012. http://www.surgeongeneral.gov/library/reports/preventing-youth-tobacco-use/exec-summary.pdf

Williams, Jean Kinney. *The U.S. Constitution.* We the People. Minneapolis: Compass Point Books, 2004.

CHAPTER SIX: **THE POWER OF MANY AND DEPTH OF KNOWLEDGE**

Michigan has a long history of using two texts with similar themes or topics in its state assessment. Two texts offer perspectives students can use to expand their thinking and deepen their understanding of a topic or theme. By encouraging a reader to adopt a different perspective, the teacher is able to support a reader in clarifying the content of a text and enable the reader to see potential alternatives to central themes. It is the basis of deconstruction, a philosophy of literary criticism that encourages the reader to use clues from structure and syntax as well as the actual content to identify central and marginal ideas in the texts.

SIDENOTE—Cynthia: My childhood was filled with the deconstruction of movies, which I have, in turn, taught my own children and my students. As noted in Chapter Four, juxtaposing two visual texts on the same topic can lead to engaging and meaningful dialogue. I was having a difficult time connecting students to ***The Canterbury Tales*** and was looking for a text that would offer students a contemporary vision of a pilgrimage. After several unsuccessful connections, I stumbled upon the movie *The Way* starring Martin Sheen. I recognized it immediately as the missing link.

The Power of Multiple Texts

Common Core State Standard 9

The Common Core recognizes the power of multiple texts with Common Core State Standard 9:

CCSS 9: Analyze how two or more texts address similar themes or topics in order to build knowledge or to compare the approaches the authors take.

Hess's Cognitive Rigor Matrix

Anyone who has developed curriculum or created thematic units is conscious of the power of multiple texts. The

Storyteller's View: Depth of Understanding

Some of our most significant insights appear in children's books because the authors understand human nature. *Charlotte's Web*, by E.B. White, focuses on our main themes for this last chapter. Charlotte is the only being in the barn willing to dig to discover that Wilbur's goodness permeates his being, and she then undertakes an advertising campaign that brings Wilbur fame because she changes public *perception* of Wilbur. He also explores his own modest capabilities, so if either of them were unwilling to work to reach the depths, they would fail, just as the superficial reader of complex text fails to gain full understanding.

To demonstrate the power of many, we might pair *Charlotte's Web* with other texts to deepen our thinking. A comparison with *The Little Red Hen* may help us understand farm life. Combining *Charlotte's Web* with a Frog and Toad book can help expand our view of friendship, and examining the strength of barn animals working together along with the stone soup fable shows the benefits of collaboration. A final, powerful pairing might be to read about the origin of spin doctors to see Charlotte as one who skillfully maneuvers her presentation to alter public perception.

ability to see multiple perspectives is an essential skill in a democratic society and a global world. *The Split History of the Civil War* by Stephanie Fitzgerald (Compass Point Books 2013) is a book that incorporates two texts written from different perspectives. It provides the Northern view and the Southern view of the Civil War. The following perspectives concern the Battle of Gettysburg.

Graphic organizers can serve as helpful tools to scaffold student thinking. Obviously, a Venn diagram would be one way to compare two perspectives. However, another way to compare two texts is through a Levels of Meaning Chart. Students are taught to use the Levels of Meaning Chart to move from the texts to the big idea or theory. This activity will put their thinking on the Cognitive Rigor Matrix at the "Analyze" level and at the DOK (Depth of Knowledge) level of 4 (Extended Thinking). Note that the analysis at this DOK level calls for two or more texts.

This chapter's focus on depth of meaning and the power of many explores three texts on the Civil War as we strive for a deep understanding of a war with a horrible price in young lives. Out of that conflict arose a battle-scarred nation that struggled to overcome its flaws.

Revised Bloom's Taxonomy	Webb's DOK Level 1 Recall & Reproduction	Webb's DOK Level 2 Basic Skills & Concepts	Webb's DOK Level 3 Strategic Thinking/ Reasoning	Webb's DOK Level 4 Extended Thinking
Analyze	• Identify whether specific information is contained in graphic representations (e.g., map, chart, table, graph, T-chart, diagram,) or text features (e.g., headings, subheadings, captions) • Decide which text structure is appropriate to audience and purpose	• Categorize/ compare literary elements, terms, facts/details, events • Identify use of literary devices • Analyze format, organization, and internal text structure (signal words, transitions, semantic cues) of different texts • Distinguish: relevant-irrelevant information; fact/ opinion • Identify characteristic text features; distinguish between texts, genres	• Analyze information within data sets or texts • Analyze interrelationships among concepts, issues, problems • Analyze or interpret author's craft (literary device, viewpoint, or potential bias) to create or critique a text • Use reasoning, planning, and evidence to support inferences	• Analyze multiple sources of evidence or multiple works by the same author or across genres, time periods, themes • Analyze complex/ abstract themes, perspectives, concepts • Gather, analyze, and organize multiple information sources • Analyze discourse styles

Two Texts and the Levels of Meaning Chart

First, students need to mine what is near the surface—note the facts/claims/arguments/evidence (just the facts) in the text. For example, read the following paragraph from Fitzgerald's text; she is presenting the Northern perspective. Find three facts.

Gettysburg (Northern Perspective)

The Union cavalry under General John Buford reached Gettysburg, Pennsylvania, June 30—just slightly ahead of the Confederates. Buford quickly took the high ground at a spot called McPherson's Ridge, just west of town. The cavalry encountered Confederate soldiers under Brigadier General James Pettigrew, but the Confederates quickly retreated. The night of June 30, Buford's scouts reported several Confederate encampments nearby. Buford knew that a battle was soon coming.

Facts

1) General John Buford was in the Union cavalry.
2) General John Buford's calvary reached Gettysburg, Pennsylvania on June 30.
3) General John Buford took the high ground at a spot called McPherson's Ridge.

The first two sentences contain three facts. It is not surprising that the reader needs to extend beyond the raw data to reach a deeper level of meaning. When you add facts upon facts to a topic, you accumulate a large database. However, databases are readily retrievable with today's technology. Thus, at this surface level, it is not surprising that students are not particularly engaged in reading, unless the facts pertain to a topic that they are fascinated by in their own lives. The first two sentences also reveal craft; for example, the author has decided to organize her text chronologically.

The reader must dig through the surface level of facts, topics, and craft to move beyond the topsoil to the next level of meaning, concepts. Below the surface of the text lies the rich mineral ore that yields semiprecious stones and occasionally a rare gem—a concept or meaty idea that challenges the reader's thinking. Lynn Erickson states that "a concept is a mental construct that is timeless, universal, and abstract" (Erickson 30) and serves as an organizing idea. In a world full of facts that one may rip from a computer just as a vulture rips its prey, students are hungry to go a deeper level. Facts fall under topics; it is possible to learn everything about a topic, given persistent effort. For example, in the previous passage, one topic might be the generals of the Civil War. But, a concept is timeless. It is not bound by history. Concepts are universal and abstract, usually represented by one or two words. They cross disciplinary lines, enabling students to see the connections between disciplines. They encourage thinking and reflection, and I have yet to meet a student who cannot be engaged in reading when he or she is constructing knowledge rather than regurgitating knowledge. For example, a concept that might emerge in the given text is conflict/cooperation. A conceptual lens nurtures the thinking and processing of knowledge that is essential for today's students. Students will face a world of conflict/cooperation; it is a concept that will impact their lives. Below is the entire passage (pages 20–21) from Fitzgerald's text of the North's perspective of the Civil War:

Gettysburg (Northern Perspective)

The Union cavalry under General John Buford reached Gettysburg, Pennsylvania, June 30—just slightly ahead of the Confederates. Buford quickly took the high ground at a spot called McPherson's Ridge, just west of town. The cavalry encountered Confederate soldiers under Brigadier General James Pettigrew, but the Confederates quickly retreated. The night of June 30, Buford's scouts reported several Confederate encampments nearby. Buford knew that a battle was soon coming.

That battle began with a shot fired by one of Buford's troops about 7:30 the morning of July 1. Between 8 and 9 a.m., the fighting began in earnest. Buford's men managed to hold off a confederate attack while Union reinforcements rushed to the scene. As thousands of Union and Confederate soldiers joined the fight, the Confederates seemed to gain the advantage. The Union forces were slowly being pushed back through Gettysburg.

Union General Meade arrived by midnight, along with troops that would ultimately number about 93,000. The men eventually would be deployed in a line 3 miles (4.8 km) long on the high ground outside of town. The Confederates attacked the afternoon of July 2. Throughout several hours of brutal fighting, the Union lines managed to hold, but just barely.

Meade's army remained dug in along Cemetery Ridge to protect their position atop Cemetery Hill, managing to hold off a Confederate assault. On July 3 the Confederates staged a massive charge, with about 12,000 men advancing on Cemetery Ridge. Union cannons blasted them as they charged, resulting in casualties of more than half the force. At the cost of about 23,000 casualties in its army, the Union had won the battle of Gettysburg—and turned the tide of the war in the East (20-21).

The northern perception of Gettysburg suggests a concept of conflict/cooperation. It also touches upon the concepts of war strategies, power imbalance, and human persistence. Students can apply these concepts to other issues of the past or to issues of the present. Concepts in the Levels of Meaning Chart (see page 108) flow into generalizations/principles, which in turn flow into theory. A theory that one can attain by examining only the Northern perspective is the following: Battles are won by greater manpower. Look at the chart on the following page to see how the Levels of Meaning Charts can lead students to deeper thinking (also available as a blank reproducible as Appendix 6a). Reaching the depth of generalizations/principles and theory is like reaching the bedrock.

A psychological theory has two key components. It must:

1. describe a behavior and
2. make predictions about future behaviors.

Levels of Meaning Chart: Civil War from the Northern Perspective

Claims/Facts/Argument/ Evidence	Topics	Concepts	Generalization/ Principle	Theories
• General John Buford, leading the Union cavalry, took high ground on June 30. • Buford's troops met Confederates under Brigadier General James Pettigrew, and they retreated. • Union soldiers fired first shot July 1 and the battle began. • Union held ground until reinforcements arrived. • Confederates gained the advantage. • Union General Meade arrived with 93,000 troops. • Confederates attacked, but Union lines held. • On July 3 the Confederates staged a major attack with 12,000 men and the Union blasted them with cannons. Half were lost to casualties. • The Union lost 23,000 men in the battle of Gettysburg. • This battle turned the tide of the war in the East.	Union Cavalry Gettysburg Confederates Union Generals of Gettysburg War Strategy	Conflict Attack Reinforcements Imbalance Persistence Power Victory	A shift in power determines victory. The high ground wins the battle. 1. Golan Heights (Israel and Syria) 2. Sky drones	Greater power is more likely to yield victory. Battles are won by superior forces.

Now let's contrast the Northern perspective passage with the Southern perspective passage from the same book:

Gettysburg (Southern Perspective)

By late June Lee's forces were in Pennsylvania. On July 1 General A.P. Hill's troops were looking for supplies near the town of Gettysburg when they clashed with Union cavalry. Two Union infantry corps soon arrived, and more Confederate infantry joined the fight. The Confederates seemed to gain the advantage, pushing the Union soldiers back toward town.

But by midnight Union reinforcements arrived by the thousands. On July 2 the fighting raged in terrible heat. Thousands of men lay dead or dying as the Confederates continued to push the enemy back and tear holes in their defenses. But at the end of the day, the Union lines still held.

The next day Lee launched what he hoped would be the decisive blow against the Union army. About 3 p.m. 12,000 troops lined up to charge the Union line on Cemetery Ridge, led by Generals George Pickett, Johnston Pettigrew, and Isaac Trimble. They were met by artillery fire that ripped through the ranks. Still the survivors pressed on, only to be met by musket fire. After less than an hour of fighting, more than 6,000 Confederate soldiers were dead, wounded, or captured. Pickett's Charge, as it came to be known, was a failure.

The Army of Northern Virginia, which had lost a total of 28,000 men during the three-day battle, was shattered. The tide of the war had turned. Still, Lee would continue the fight for two more years (20-21).

View the Levels of Meaning Chart for the Southern perspective below.

Levels of Meaning Chart: Civil War from the Southern Perspective

Claims/Facts/Argument/Evidence	Topics	Concepts	Generalization/ Principle	Theories
• On July 1, General A.P. Hill's troops looked for supplies near Gettysburg. • They clashed with Union cavalry. • Two Union infantry corps arrived. • Confederates gained, pushing back the Union soldiers. • Midnight Union reinforcements arrived by the thousands. • Ten thousand men lay dead or dying as the Confederates continued to push the Union back. • Union lines held. • Lee launched an attack of 12,000 soldiers the next day. • After less than an hour, 6,000 Confederate soldiers were dead, wounded, or captured. • Pickett's Charge was known as a failure. • The Confederate army had lost 28,000 men during the three-day battle. The war had turned, but Lee continued to fight for two more years.	Union Confederate Gettysburg Confederate Generals Civil War	Conflict Direct Confrontation Persistence Imbalance of Power	Persistence against an imbalance of power creates victims.	Persistence cannot overcome an imbalance of power. Battles are won by persistence.

The selected texts look at the same topic from two different perspectives. The author, Fitzgerald, told the story from the perspective of how the North would describe the Battle of Gettysburg, and then she told how the South would describe the Battle of Gettysburg. When these two perspectives are analyzed on the Levels of Meaning Chart and taken to the principle or theory level of thinking, two different theories of how to win a battle emerge: The North brought in more reinforcements to cause an imbalance of power, and the South used persistence to keep the war going.

The Common Core State Standard 9 states: *Analyze how two or more texts address similar themes or topics in order to build knowledge or to compare the approaches the authors take.* With the example we have provided, students could be asked to write a constructed response comparing the two theories of how to win the battle waged at Gettysburg. The constructed responses could be scored on a rubric that expected students to delineate and compare the two theories, giving evidence from the two texts.

To move this task to opinion and use of outside or prior knowledge, students would reflect upon these theories of conflict and then apply that to what they know in today's world. For example, the North won with manpower; it kept bringing in reinforcements. However, in today's world, is conflict settled with manpower? Perhaps conflict is settled with technology, e.g., drones. Perhaps the imbalance of power is still critical, but what is considered power has literally evolved from humans.

Levels of Meaning and the Gettysburg Address

A third text on the Battle of Gettysburg from yet a different perspective could add to students' thinking. For example, the Gettysburg Address adds another perspective and richer soil, given the complexity of the text. The Levels of Meaning Chart applies the four questions to the Gettysburg Address.

Gettysburg Address

Fourscore and seven years ago our fathers brought forth on this continent a new nation, conceived in liberty and dedicated to the proposition that all men are created equal.

Now we are engaged in a great civil war, testing whether that nation or any nation so conceived and so dedicated can long endure. We are met on a great battlefield of that war. We have come to dedicate a portion of that field as a final resting-place for those who here gave their lives that that nation might live. It is altogether fitting and proper that we should do this.

But in a larger sense, we cannot dedicate, we cannot consecrate, we cannot hallow this ground. The brave men, living and dead who struggled here have consecrated it far above our poor power to add or detract. The world will little note nor long remember what we say here, but it can never forget what they did here. It is for us the living rather to be dedicated here to the unfinished work which they who fought here have thus far so nobly advanced. It is rather for us to be here dedicated to the great task remaining before us—that from these honored dead we take increased devotion to that cause for which they gave the last full measure of devotion—that we here highly resolve that these dead shall not have died in vain, that this nation under God shall have a new birth of freedom, and that government of the people, by the people, for the people shall not perish from the earth (Lincoln).

Levels of Meaning Chart: Gettysburg Address

Claims/Facts/Argument/Evidence	Topics	Concepts	Generalization/ Principle	Theories
• Four score and seven years ago our fathers brought forth, upon this continent, a new nation. • A nation conceived of Liberty and • dedicated to the proposition that all men are created equal. • Now we are engaged in a great civil war. • We are met here on a great battlefield of that war. • We have come to dedicate a portion of it as a final resting place for those who here gave their lives that that nation might live. • The world will little note, nor long remember, what we say here, but can never forget what they did here. • ...we here highly resolve that these dead shall not have died in vain; that this nation shall have a new birth of freedom; and that this government of the people, by the people, for the people, shall not perish from the earth.	American Revolutionary War American Civil War Battle of Gettysburg Constitution Government We the People	History War Democracy Language or Rhetoric Opportunity Citizenship Sacrifice Liberty Freedom Sacrifice Change/ Continuity Death Birth	Freedom is achieved through the inequality of sacrifices. Democracy exists if people are willing to sacrifice to secure the rights of citizens. Democracy is dedicated to the equality of men but survives on the inequality of lives.	Sacrifice may result in opportunity.

Lincoln perceived the battle through the conceptual lens of change/continuity. He recognized the cost and sacrifice of the men, but the continuity of liberty was the result: the birth of a new nation. He saw the battle and the war as a means to an end. The other two texts were basically an account of the events of the battles. Although the first two texts reported events of the battle from two different points of view, they both were without the perspective of time and space. The third text reflects on the events from a distance of space, time, and position.

Disparate Text and the Levels of Meaning Chart

In this time of Google, students can gain information on anything, and the source is as close as their phones. With students that would be very close and ready. The premium of education is no longer preparation to be a contestant on *Jeopardy*. It is no longer what you know, but what you can do with what you know. This is the reason new reading standards (CCSS) for college and career readiness feature process (thinking) vs. content.

Reading to the core means that students read text carefully to determine the message of the author. They read critically to analyze for perspective and purpose by inspecting the text for craft, structure, and language. This includes auditory and visual texts. They create by synthesizing text to gain new insights, new knowledge, new voice, new perspective—that is what is really "new" about CCSS. And this is what is essential for college and career readiness.

Sidenote—Elaine: In the 2006–2007 school year, the Michigan Department of Education purchased my time from the Macomb ISD to develop model literature units that met the new (at that time) high school English/language arts standards. The "Close and Critical Reading Questions," along with the "Essential Questions," shaped the thinking to be used with the collection of texts that all fit into a theme or big idea. We intentionally selected text that would cause cognitive dissonance or disequilibrium so that students had to work to make the connections to make the experience generative. In the unit that featured *Night*, the big idea was survival. In order for students to gain new insights or knowledge about survival, we offered students information about cockroaches, which are the oldest surviving insects. Our intention was that by comparing what author Elie Wiesel did to survive and how cockroaches have survived millions of years, students would have new insights about survival.

The final level in the Levels of Meaning Chart is theories. Comparing theories across two or more pieces of text brings the student to theme or big idea thinking. To extend this concept even further, generative thinking is often encouraged with a disparate text, which can cause cognitive disequilibrium. A disparate text that shares a concept with several other texts but is from another discipline is likely to cause conflict with a student's current beliefs or stretch his/her beliefs/knowledge/thinking. In an attempt to seek consonance, new knowledge can result from the interplay between the reader and the texts. For example, place the Gettysburg Address next to the following "Response of Vegetation to Wildfire" text and ask students to find connections between the two. Students can use the Levels of Meaning Chart to find concepts that are similar and will struggle to create new knowledge, either through assimilation or accommodation.

Disparate Text: "Response of Vegetation to Wildfire"

Various plant species depend upon fire as a means to reproduce, while others have adapted to survive in the presence of fire. However, the process by which species have adapted varies greatly. Species such as Monterey, Bishop, and Knobcone pines have adapted to produce pine cones which hold seeds locked by a resinous coating that is melted away by fire (Baker 1971). Following a fire the seeds are released and benefit from improved growing conditions such as available sunlight, a seedbed of bare mineral soil, and nutrients released from organic matter cleared by the fire. Other species of plants produce seeds which lie dormant in the seedbed and will germinate only after a fire heat-treats their seed coat and removes duff from the top soil.

In the case of Coast Live Oaks, *stump sprouting*, or the generation of new stems and growth from burnt trunks and branches, occurs following a blaze. In similar manner species such as Our Lord's Candle, *Yucca whipplei*, produce new growth from the root crown of a burnt plant in a process known as *crown sprouting*. Although all plant communities have developed a response to fire, the chaparral community associated with the Mediterranean climates of the world may be the most fire responsive (Ainsworth and Doss 1).

Levels of Meaning: "Response of Vegetation to Wildfire"

Claims/Facts/Argument/Evidence	Topics	Concepts	Generalization/ Principle	Theories
• Various plant species depend upon fire as a means to reproduce. • Some plant species have adapted to survive in the presence of fire. • Species such as Monterey, Bishop, and Knobcone pines have adapted to produce pine cones which hold seeds locked by a resinous coating that is melted away by fire. • In Coast Live Oaks, *stump sprouting*, or the generation of new stems and growth from burnt trunks and branches, occurs following a blaze. • Our Lord's Candle, *Yucca whipplei*, produces new growth from the root crown of a burnt plant in a process known as *crown sprouting*.	Plant Species Stump and Crown Sprouting New Growth Wildfire Vegetation	Opportunity Life Cycle Change/ Continuity	The cycle of life moves from death to life to death to life.	Out of the sacrificial ashes springs new life.

Text: "Response of Vegetation to Wildfire" and The Gettysburg Address

Both the Gettysburg Address and "Response of Vegetation to Wildfire" share a concept: change/ continuity. Lincoln states:

- "...our fathers brought forth, upon this continent, a new nation, conceived in Liberty..."
- "...those who gave their lives that our nation might live."
- "...we here highly resolve that these dead shall not have died in vain..."
- "...this nation shall have a new birth of freedom..."

The "Response of Vegetation to Wildfire" states:

- "...seeds locked by a resinous coating that is melted away by fire."
- "...seeds which lie dormant in the seedbed and will germinate only after a fire heat-treats their seed coat and removes duff from the top soil."

- "...generation of new stems and growth from burnt trunks and branches..."
- "...produce new growth from the root crown of a burnt plant..."

The "resinous coating" is the obsolete structure of power; both need to be dissolved to release new life, whether it is a government or a forest. One could expand it to include the death of monarchy to the creation of a republic or to the ending of modernism to make way for post-modernism. We had the Dark Ages, which led to a renaissance of enlightenment, and, as a result of the Civil War, we had the birth of a new definition of democracy.

If we are to prepare our students for the twenty-first century, we must create readers capable of synthesizing. The twenty-first century will require the next generation to expand beyond the re-telling of events or data. They must be able to read the word and the world. As readers, they will need to create new knowledge, see multiple perspectives, and accommodate into their existing schema the constant influx of new ideas. The global world will flourish only if we have citizens who are creative readers and thinkers.

Cognitive Rigor Matrix "Create" Level

Revised Bloom's Taxonomy	Webb's DOK Level 1 Recall & Reproduction	Webb's DOK Level 2 Basic Skills & Concepts	Webb's DOK Level 3 Strategic Thinking/ Reasoning	Webb's DOK Level 4 Extended Thinking
Reorganize elements into new patterns/ structures; generate; hypothesize; design; plan; and produce.	Brainstorm ideas, concepts, problems, or perspectives related to a topic or concept.	Generate conjectures or hypotheses based on observation or prior knowledge and experience.	• Synthesize information within one source or text. • Develop a complex model for a given situation. • Develop an alternative solution.	• Synthesize information across multiple sources or texts. • Articulate a new voice, alternate theme, and new knowledge or perspective.

This kind of reading and thinking goes to the highest or deepest level on Hess's Cognitive Rigor Matrix.

Questions for Multiple Texts

To date, we have not had a way to measure this kind of reading and thinking on a standardized assessment. Expectations to read text to create and synthesize information will have to come from curricular objectives, local assessments, classroom instruction, or school improvement plans, etc. We considered modifying the questions to accommodate multiple texts to push students' thinking to the synthesize/create level. The modified questions would be as follows:

- What is the parallel message in the two texts? *(Sacrifice for new life: fire that destroys the tree frees the seeds to grow, and the demise of the old system of democracy creates a need for a "new birth of a nation.")*
- How does each text say it? *(Political speech and science article)*
- What is the principle, generalization, or theory shared by the texts? *(Death promotes a new beginning.)*

- What insights or new knowledge did the texts render?
    - o "...seeds locked by a resinous coating that is melted away by fire." *(Old ways of democracy were melted away by war.)*
    - o "...seeds which lie dormant in the seedbed and will germinate only after a fire heat-treats their seed coat and removes duff from the top soil." *(A new citizenry will flourish after the demise of the old regime.)*
    - o "...generation of new stems and growth from burnt trunks and branches...." *(New technology replaced slave labor.)*
    - o "...produce new growth from the root crown of a burnt plant...." *(A new nation will emerge from the ruins of the war.)*

Close and Critical Reading Sample Answers

What does the text say? (Briefly summarize the Gettysburg Address at the literal level.) Our nation was conceived 87 years ago. The new nation was born in liberty and based on the premise that all men were equal. However, we are now involved in a civil war challenging those assumptions. We meet on a battlefield of this war to dedicate a part of the land to lay soldiers' bodies in rest. It is right that we do this act. Yet, the land is already made holy by the men who have died here for the sake of the nation's unity. The world will not remember us or our words, but they will remember the men who fought here. It is up to the living to finish the work of those who have died. So, we pledge here that this government/nation shall not die but be reborn in freedom and the people's government shall not perish.

How does it say it? In other words, how does the author develop the text to convey his/her purpose? (What are the genre, format, organization, features, etc.?) The **title** of the text is Gettysburg Address. The title is named after the place where the speech was given: Gettysburg. The author uses **archaic words**: "fourscore and seven years ago." A score means 20 years, but it is not a common word in contemporary times. The author uses **first-person plural**: "our fathers." First person places the speaker on par with the audience, and a commonality is established. In fact, "our fathers" encourages the concept that we are all family/brothers. The author uses **personification** by capitalizing the word "Liberty." The author's **genre** is speech and he employs a religious **motif** to emphasize the sacredness of the moment by using words such as "consecrate," "devotion," and "new birth." Burial is one of the sacraments of the church. The **tone** is solemn; it is given at a mass gravesite. The author uses the **repetition of words/phrases** to emphasize his point: "we can not dedicate—we can not consecrate—we can not hallow this ground." The word "nation" is noted five times. The author uses **contrast**. He contrasts the dead/death ("gave their lives") with the living/life ("that our nation might live"). The author's **conclusion** incorporates a **call to action**: "It is for us, the living, rather to be dedicated here to the unfinished work which they have, thus far, so nobly carried on". The **lead** is a **historical allusion** to the Revolutionary War and 1776 and contains an **intertextual allusion** to the Declaration of Independence, e.g., "all men are created equal." The author effectively uses transitional phrases/words: "But" and "it is rather for us." The author also **contrasts/compares** the impact of words versus actions. The author refers to the Declaration of Independence, and the words "all men are created equal" are woven into his text. Consequently, the words of the previous era continue to live, and the concept lives. So, when the author notes, "The world will little note, nor long remember, what we say here, but can never forget what they did here," one wonders if the author is not very aware of the power of words. He uses the repetition of simple words to convey a powerful concept to represent democracy at the end of his speech, "This government of the people, by the people, for the people, shall not perish from the earth."

What does the text mean? (What message, concepts, generalizations/principles (themes), and theories is the author trying to get across?) Note that there are multiple messages in a text: Each generation stands upon the shoulders/feats/actions of its ancestors, but the struggle continues, and if the goal is to be safeguarded, then the present generation must rededicate and sacrifice itself to its purpose. Another message might be that each generation builds upon the prior generation in the hope of maintaining the legacy it inherited.

So, what? (How does the meaning of the text relate to me, to other texts, and/or to the world?) I am reminded of F. Scott Fitzgerald's book *The Great Gatsby*. The book ends with Nick, the narrator, noting the constant struggle against the current. Though he notes that he is pushed back, he also believes that someday the shore will be attainable. Nick believes in the possibilities of the American Dream.

Young people today are continuing the struggle. The Dream Defenders "is a sustainable network of youth and student leaders" (Dream Defenders) who believe that "nonviolence, love, and unity will always triumph over racism and hate" (Dream Defenders). Young leaders such as these are heirs to Abraham Lincoln's "government of the people, by the people, for the people." The Dream Defenders refuse to be denied their inheritance and are willing to sacrifice and rededicate themselves to their forefathers' goal. So, I have to ask myself, "What have I inherited from my ancestors that I am willing to sacrifice and rededicate myself to for the sake of the next generation?"

Chapter Six Works Cited

Ainsworth, Jack, and Troy Alan Doss. "Natural History of Fire and Flood Cycles." California Coastal Commission. 18 August 1995. Web. 14 July 2013.

Dream Defenders. "About Us." *Dream Defenders*. n.d. Web. 23 October 2013.

Erickson, H. Lynn. *Stirring the Head, Heart, and Soul: Redefining Curriculum, Instruction, and Concept-Based Learning.* 3rd Edition. Thousand Oaks, CA: Corwin Press, 2008.

Fitzgerald, Stephanie. *The Split History of the Civil War.* Stevens Point, WI. Compass Point Books, A Capstone Imprint, 2013.

Hess, Karen K. "Hess's Cognitive Rigor Matrix." National Center for the Improvement of Educational Assessment. 2011. Web. 13 July 2013.

Lincoln, Abraham. "Gettysburg Address." Avalon Project: Documents in Law, History, and Diplomacy. Lillian Goldman Law Library. Yale Law School. 2008. Web. 27 August 2013.

CHAPTER SEVEN: **EXPECTATIONS OF A TWENTY-FIRST CENTURY CITIZEN**

Read, Read, Read

A skill is acquired through practice. Literacy, like any skill one wants to develop, requires practice, practice, practice. Doing so captures Common Core Anchor Standard 10 for Reading: *"Read and comprehend complex literary and informational texts independently and proficiently."*

Though it is not explicitly stated in the anchor standard, it is assumed that students are reading at their grade level or beyond. Furthermore, it is assumed students are reading complex text that increases in difficulty each year and complements the escalating informational text reading requirements. To achieve this standard, the Common Core literature advocates a "staircase" of increasing text complexity. At each grade level, students read at their grade level and stretch into the next grade level. This system assumes that students are reading enough at each level to develop and refine the skill.

A 2004 report by the National Endowment for the Arts, a compilation of 40 studies by universities, foundations, business groups, and government agencies, revealed "plummeting levels of reading among young people over the past two decades" (Mehegan 1). In addition, they found that only 30 percent of 13-year-olds read almost every day, and students who never read for pleasure doubled from 1984 to 2004 (Mehegan 1).

The National Endowment for the Arts is not the only institute reporting disturbing reading/literacy statistics. Their statistics simply support the future awaiting these students if they are unable to acquire the literacy skills they need for the twenty-first century.

- "Thirty-four million adults function at below basic literacy levels, meaning they are unable to complete simple literacy tasks such as filling out a job application, filling out a deposit slip, or reading a prescription label" (National Commission on Adult Literacy 2003 1).
- "The U.S. is the only country among 20 OECD free-market countries where the current generation is less well educated than the previous one" (National Commission on Adult Literacy 2008 1).
- "Approximately one in eight children in the United States never graduates from high school. Based on calculations per school day (180 days of seven hours each), one high school student drops out every nine seconds" (Lehr, Johnson, Bremer, Cosio, & Thompson 1).
- "Every year, one in three young adults—more than 1.2 million people—drop out of high school" (National Commission on Adult Literacy 2008 1).

It is obvious the cost is too high to continue witnessing the decline of reading; it is essential we awaken students to the possibilities reading provides, the possible lives they can pursue if they are armed with literacy. One of the most disturbing statistics we ran across while researching this chapter was published in 2008 by the National Commission on Adult Literacy: "One in every

100 U.S. adults 16 and older is in prison or jail in America (about 2.3 million in 2006). About 43 percent do not have a high school diploma or equivalent, and 56 percent have very low literacy skills."

Literacy is a family problem, a community problem, and a national problem. Given the changing world, it is also a global problem. This chapter suggests possible places to start. But, before we start offering ideas, let's review a few more facts to emphasize the need.

Penny Kittle, teacher, professional developer, and author, did her own research on student reading. Through video interviews with high school students (See Penny Kittle's website, and view "Reading 2011" under the Videos section), Kittle quickly revealed that many students did not participate in required reading and did not read for enjoyment. In fact, they just didn't read by conscious choice. She did discover the majority of students used survival techniques (class discussions, summaries of novels, CliffsNotes) to get through their courses. She wondered if these had been their strategies prior to high school. Not surprisingly, she discovered that the students had not read in middle school either. So, a life void of reading was not a phenomena exclusive to high school students; there was a long pattern to this behavior. Kittle's search uncovered that college students read between 200 and 600 pages a week. This is a lot of pages, if you are not reading at all. It also provides insight into the disturbing statistics of *The American Dream 2.0 Report*. As of 2013, the college dropout rate includes the following:

- Forty-six percent of those who enter a U.S. college fail to graduate within six years.
- Only 37 percent of African-Americans graduate within six years.
- Only 42 percent of Hispanic students graduate within six years (HCM Strategists 5).

As noted before, this is a systemic problem. Students are not reading early in their academic careers. It is no wonder they are often unprepared for the reading required in college. According to NAEP, more than 60 percent of middle and high school students scored below the proficient level in reading achievement (U.S. Department of Education National Center for Educational Statistics). These results reveal that millions of young people cannot understand or evaluate text, provide relevant details, or support inferences about the written documents they read. Many of these students' reading levels are so low that they cannot even read (decode) the text.

To compound the challenge, the Common Core has raised the ante. New standards have caused Lexile levels to be increased at each grade level.

Text Complexity Grade Band in the Standards	Old Lexile Ranges	Lexile Ranges Aligned to CCR Expectations
K–1	N/A	N/A
2–3	450–725	450–790
4–5	645–845	770–980
6–8	860–1010	955–1155
9–10	960–1115	1080–1305
11–CCR	1070–1220	1215–1355

Closing the Literacy Gap

Even without these last few pages of statistics, most teachers would agree reading is a problem for the majority of their students. We know the problem. We are looking for answers. How can one ensure that all students are reading at the required Lexile and complexity levels?

Obviously, we do not have a magic pill. However, we do have some ideas. We need a system that collects data on students' literacy skills. Not only should data be obtained and recorded, but it should also be communicated to all stakeholders: student, teachers, and parents. Obviously, teachers need to know the levels of literacy skill development for all the students they serve. Only then will they be able to develop a plan of action and initiate a literacy plan. But, as noted before, the literacy of one child impacts us all. So, students need to know where they are functioning with literacy so:

- they can set realistic goals and
- initiate plans to practice and grow.

Parents need to know where their child is functioning so:

- they can offer necessary support—for example, homework—and
- support their child's literacy goals.

SIDENOTE—Elaine: Much of my work is done with what are called "high priority" high schools, where many students have limited literacy skills. Most of the schools give an assessment to determine the reading levels of the students, but the scores are rarely shared with the teaching staff or the students. It always surprises me. They both need this information to move forward. I can only think, "What if my doctor treated me without information on my blood pressure and cholesterol levels?"

A crucial component of a literacy plan is student responsibility. Students need to be invested in their reading. Recently, responsibility for student reading growth has focused on the teacher. It is a fair focus. But, the teacher will only be able to show reading improvement if he is able to instill in a student a sense of commitment to the task. Parents can support the reading, but ultimately a student must be invested.

Student literacy profiles are one way to cultivate student responsibility. Three times a year, a student's reading could be assessed at a grade level and a Lexile level. The fall assessment provides the teacher, student, and parents a baseline by which to determine goals. The winter assessment monitors the student's progress and allows the student an opportunity for reflection and reassessment of initial goals. The spring assessment provides the student feedback on her growth. The student maintains her literacy profile; it can easily be stored in a manila folder in a class file drawer or cardboard box. The teacher maintains a class folder for her records that he can use to provide data to document the effectiveness of his instruction. It is assumed the teacher would provide a student reading below grade level the appropriate instruction and practice needed to increase the student's reading skills, resulting in a student attaining a higher grade level and Lexile level.

Reading Lexile Record—Student Copy

Reading	Fall	Winter	Spring
Reading Grade Level or Lexile Level	Grade _______ Lexile _______	Grade _______ Lexile _______	Grade _______ Lexile _______

Classroom Teacher Copy

Student Name	Fall	Winter	Spring
Jane Doe	Grade _______ Lexile _______	Grade _______ Lexile _______	Grade _______ Lexile _______
Etc.	Grade _______ Lexile _______	Grade _______ Lexile _______	Grade _______ Lexile _______

Focusing on Fluency for Proficiency

Reading fluency is a crucial component of reading. It has always been a focus of instruction with developing readers at the elementary and beginning middle school grades. However, seldom was reading fluency connected to high school instruction. A new study by David D. Paige, Timothy V. Rasinski, and Theresa Magpuri-Lavell reframe prior perceptions. Their article in the *Journal of Adolescent & Adult Literacy*, "Is Fluent, Expressive Reading Important for High School Readers?" strongly supports the necessity of focusing on fluency at the high school level.

The authors devote attention to the power of prosody, an aspect of reading fluency that is often ignored, especially with older students. Prosody is the use of rhythm, tempo, pitch, emphasis, etc., in speech. It is how the speaker uses his voice to convey meaning. Prosody is intricately linked to fluency and comprehension. How can a reader comprehend or be fluent if she reads internally or externally in a monotone? It is the voice in your head or in my ear that enables you to reach deeper levels of comprehension.

There are a variety of activities one can use to nurture prosody. For example, take a sentence and place emphasis on different words. When the reader or speaker emphasizes one word over another, it impacts the meaning of the sentence. Emphasize the bold words below and listen with your ear.

- Cynthia likes **RACOONS**.
- **CYNTHIA** likes raccoons.

Prosody also conveys emotional states, levels of interest, etc. President Franklin D. Roosevelt's first fireside chat is a wonderful example of the power of prosody. He was addressing an America in panic, yet he was able to convey comfort, warmth, and security through his inflections. Read a phrase from his chat: **"I shall continue to have your cooperation..."** Now, read the same phrase as:

- a frightened citizen
- Roosevelt trying to calm the nation
- a professor lecturing
- a parent explaining to a child

It is easy to see the possible activities one could develop in the classroom to nurture prosody. The activities could encourage the rereading of texts and encourage a closer and more critical reading of the texts.

Reading with expression or prosody is a trait of a proficient and fluid reader. It is a trait we have too often assumed all students possess by high school. Not surprisingly, the study by Paige, Rasinski, and Magpuri-Lavell revealed that ninth-grade students with the highest levels of prosody were the same students with the highest levels of reading comprehension. What was surprising was the revelation that oral-reading prosody is related to silent-reading comprehension for secondary students. The researchers discovered that a significant number of students had prosody levels well below expectations. Thus, they brought to light another element of fluency that must be addressed at the secondary level.

SIDENOTE—Cynthia: Writing this book has been humbling. I had always thought that I was exceptional at teaching Shakespeare. Now I realize that my students had so much success with delving the depths of Shakespeare not because of me, but rather because of my emphasis on prosody during the text. We read the text, we play with emphasis, and we watch the text. I have always known a play should be heard. Yet, I know prosody is a crucial component in fluency; it keeps me reading. It is the voice or voices that spring from the written word and create dialogue inside my head. It is the voice and/or voices that I often talk back to on paper or in my invisible thoughts.

Monitoring Fluency

Prosody is one of the components of reading fluency; but it is not the only component. The components of reading fluency are as follows:

- **Accuracy** concerns a reader's skill at decoding the words in the text he or she reads (Rasinski et al. 294).
- **Rate** relates to a reader's level of "automaticity" in recognizing words (Rasinski et al. 295).
- **Prosody** concerns a reader's skill at making oral reading sound like real speech (Rasinski et al. 293).

Though research will continue, there is no doubt that there is a relationship between prosody and comprehension. Further research will only add to the dialogue and constructed knowledge of reading.

Finally, reading comprehension and close and critical reading have been a primary focus of this text. It is a crucial skill for a twenty-first-century citizen. Reading comprehension also needs to be monitored and measured in the student literacy profile.

Teachers can monitor fluency over a year to show growth, and once more, the student needs to be actively engaged in the data collection. Note that the previous student profile on Lexile level is slowly expanding to include more information—reading fluency rate, oral reading fluency traits, and reading comprehension.

Student Literacy Profile

Name:		**Grade:**	
Reading	**Fall**	**Winter**	**Spring**
Reading Grade Level or Lexile Level	Grade _______ Lexile _______	Grade _______ Lexile _______	Grade _______ Lexile _______
Reading Fluency Rate	Oral Rate _______ Silent Rate _______	Oral Rate _______ Silent Rate _______	Oral Rate _______ Silent Rate _______
Oral Reading Fluency Traits	Expression and Volume _______ Phrasing _______ Smoothness _______ Pace _______	Expression and Volume _______ Phrasing _______ Smoothness _______ Pace _______	Expression and Volume _______ Phrasing _______ Smoothness _______ Pace _______
Reading Comprehension with a Single Text	Grade level of text _______ Subject of text _____ _______________	Grade level of text _______ Subject of text _____ _______________	Grade level of text _______ Subject of text _____ _______________
Provide a summary of the text.	Summary Rubric Score _______	Summary Rubric Score _______	Summary Rubric Score _______
Analyze text for craft, perspective and structure.	Text Analysis Rubric Score _______	Text Analysis Rubric Score _______	Text Analysis Rubric Score _______
Identify the theme or big idea of the text.	Theme or Big Idea Rubric Score _______	Theme or Big Idea Rubric Score _______	Theme or Big Idea Rubric Score _______
Delineate and evaluate the argument.	Argument Rubric Score _______	Argument Rubric Score _______	Argument Rubric Score _______
Analyze visual text.	Visual Text Rubric Score _______	Visual Text Rubric Score _______	Visual Text Rubric Score _______
Four-question Score • What does the text say? • How does the text say it? • What does it mean? • So, what?	Four Questions Rubric Score _______	Four Questions Rubric Score _______	Four Questions Rubric Score _______

For more instructional activities and assessments, go to the Michigan's Mission Possible website. Scroll down to Literacy in Action (Module 5). There you will find resources for a variety of reading levels.

Final Component: Performance Task

Current literature defines performance tasks as an approach to the monitoring of students' progress in relationship to identified learner outcomes. In other words, performance tasks require the student to create answers or products that demonstrate their knowledge or skills.

Characteristics of an Effective Performance Assessment Task

Teachers are capable of writing performance tasks. In fact, they should write performance tasks for their classes. Teachers will be more comfortable with the future assessments they will be evaluated with by their administrators, and students will be more comfortable with the assessments they are facing in high-stakes testing. In addition, teacher performance tasks can enrich their current curriculum. The Office of Technology Assessment of the U.S. Congress defines performance assessment as "any form of testing that requires a student to create an answer or a product that demonstrates his or her knowledge skills."

A teacher needs to consider the following when creating a performance task:

- Develop tasks that are meaningful and require the use of skills and knowledge acquired prior to the assessment.
- Create a performance task that has multiple facets that are all measureable.
- Present students with clearly stated outcomes and the evaluation tools to be used for measurement. The students must be aware of the expectations.

CCSS delineate assessments as performance tasks that require students to read, watch, and/or listen to text in preparation for either writing or speaking performance.

So, students demonstrate their knowledge through one or more of the following performances.

- Speaking
- Using one of three modes of written discourse:
  1. Argument
  2. Informational/explanatory
  3. Narrative

It is important to note that students do not just spring to the performance task. Rather, students are provided with the opportunity to act upon a series of smaller performances prior to the final assessment.

Let's Try One

Keeping to the theme of an educated citizenry, an example of a performance task with a series of constructed responses/steps could be as follows:

Read the excerpt from the Declaration of Independence. Answer the four questions:

1. What does the text say?
2. How does the text say it?
3. What does it mean?
4. So, what?

Or,

- Read the Preamble to the Constitution of the United States. What similarities does it share with the Pledge of Allegiance?
- Through a series of smaller tasks, the student is finally presented with a cumulative performance task such as the following: Read the following texts: an excerpt from the Declaration of Independence, the third article of the Articles of Confederation, the Preamble to the Constitution of the United States of America, and the Pledge of Allegiance. Each either states or implies promises for a better life. Write a constructed response comparing the promises and the conditions prompting these promises. Use evidence from the text to support your analysis.

Or,

- Read and analyze the following texts: an excerpt from the Declaration of Independence, the third article of the Articles of Confederation, the Preamble to the Constitution of the United States of America, and the Pledge of Allegiance. Write an essay in which you address the texts' primary concern. Support your position with evidence from the texts. Be sure to acknowledge and support with textual evidence any competing views presented by the texts.

Remember, even with identical texts, there are a multitude of constructed responses and performance tasks a teacher can create for an assessment. The four texts used in these performance tasks are provided as follows:

Declaration of Independence Excerpt

We hold these truths to be self-evident, that all men are created equal, that they are endowed by their Creator with certain unalienable rights, that among these are life, liberty and the pursuit of happiness. That to secure these rights, governments are instituted among men, deriving their just powers from the consent of the governed. That whenever any form of government becomes destructive to these ends, it is the right of the people to alter or to abolish it, and to institute new government, laying its foundation on such principles and organizing its powers in such form, as to them shall seem most likely to effect their safety and happiness.

Articles of Confederation Article III

The said States hereby severally enter into a firm league of friendship with each other, for their common defense, the security of their liberties, and their mutual and general welfare, binding themselves to assist each other, against all force offered to, or attacks made upon them, or any of them, on account of religion, sovereignty, trade, or any other pretense whatever.

Preamble to the Constitution

We the People of the United States, in Order to form a more perfect Union, establish justice, insure domestic Tranquility, provide for the common defense, promote the general Welfare, and secure the Blessings of Liberty to ourselves and our Posterity, do ordain and establish this Constitution for the United States of America.

Pledge of Allegiance

I Pledge Allegiance to the flag
of the United States of America
and to the Republic
for which it stands,
one Nation under God,
indivisible,
with liberty and justice for all.

Assessment Rubric

The teacher must decide prior to writing the performance task what she is requiring of the students. The use of multiple texts is an opportunity for students to gather, analyze, and integrate information. The use of one or more texts is an opportunity to evaluate the credibility, completeness, relevancy, and accuracy of sources. Once the teacher determines the skill or skills being assessed, then she must also determine the product to be created. Note that the product is often a writing assignment that provides the teacher an opportunity to assess CCSS writing standards.

It is possible to and essential that we develop and incorporate performance tasks in our classrooms that effectively assess students' skills and measure students' readiness for college and careers. Teachers are professionals, and we can create meaningful assessments that will complement our curriculum and provide evidence of student growth. Examples of middle school and high school performance tasks and the rubrics used to score them are available on the Reading to the Core website. (Search for "Reading to the Core.") We have found collaboration to be a powerful source of ideas and would strongly recommend the creation of performance tasks by a department as a worthwhile series of professional development days.

Performance task feedback is essential for students. Each student needs to know where he is at in his literacy journey. In fact, the necessity of student involvement cannot be emphasized enough. The apathy many students feel toward literacy must be bridged if we are to maintain our democracy. An educated citizenry was recognized as essential by our founding fathers; it is woven into the fabric of our nation. In 1787, Thomas Jefferson wrote to James Madison, "Above all things I hope the education of the common people will be attended to; convinced that on their good sense we may rely with the most security for the preservation of a due degree of liberty" (Jefferson Letter 3). Jefferson and Adams recognized the essential role education would play in a democracy. We, as teachers, are the custodians of this sacred trust.

A Shared Vision

The world has changed rapidly. The Constitution of the United States has added amendments to deal with the rapid change. The judicial system has dealt with that rapid change through its interpretation of the law. Corporations and organizations that could not change quickly became extinct. It is time for public education to develop a vision or "re-vision" of itself as an organization. Peter Senge, a founding chair of the Society for Organizational Learning (SOL), has researched successful organizations. He has noted the generative nature of a shared vision: as one that becomes easier to understand as people talk, and as it becomes clearer, people become more positive about its advantages (Senge 227).

We have suggested that our vision is one of an educated citizenry for the twenty-first century. So, how do we share this vision of literacy? How do we clarify the benefits? We start with the student and determine the student's needs. We share the findings and the knowledge with the student. The following chart is a visual representation of the starting point for a shared vision.

Shared Literacy Vision for the Future

Literacy

Where students are now:

•
•
•
•
•
•
•
•
•
•
•

Strategies:

- Complex Text
- Visual Text
- Guided Highlighted Reading
- Mining Maps
- Card Games
- Levels of Meaning Chart
- Videos
- Websites
- Assessment Rubrics
- Constructed Responses
- Performance Tasks
- Literacy Profiles
- Four Questions
- Text-dependent Questions
- Summaries
- Text Explication
- Author's Craft Activities
- Cognitive Rigor Matrix

Vision for the Future

- Reads fluently at grade level
- Reads with prosody
- Summarizes text (print and visual)
- Analyzes author's craft (print and visual)
- Delineates and evaluates argument in text (print and visual)
- Analyzes multiple and diverse text for presentation and content
- Reads and resolves disparate text to find theme, principles, and theory

Yet, it is more than students. Yes, students must be invested in their learning. But, they cannot stand alone. The community, government, parents, and teachers must be invested in student learning. Together we must construct a shared vision of a literate citizen. As Senge suggests, sharing a vision includes finding views of the future that people share that encourage true commitment instead of just going along. As leaders become more skilled at this, they learn just how negative the practice of dictating a vision is—even though it may be a deep, sincere belief (Senge 9).

In recent years, the vision has felt dictated. But, it doesn't have to be. We can create a shared vision of literacy. In fact, we must construct a shared vision of literacy if we are to create literate citizens for the twenty-first century; our democracy depends on it. Close, critical, and generative readers are vital for our democracy. We cannot imagine every crisis our students will face in the future. We do know that they will face issues involving equality, poverty, education, personal liberties, etc. We do know they will need to be aware of their world and their government if they are to be active and informed participants in their government. Democracy is fragile; our challenge is to give our students the tools they will need to safeguard its existence.

Storyteller's View: Conclusion

We have wound our way through many layers to the core of complex text. The core meaning in complex text, a magical blend of content and craft, brings us the sterling "aha! moments" we eagerly seek for ourselves and our students.

Our journey began with our focus on global citizenship and our sense of commitment to changing the disheartening NAEP statistics on student knowledge and the lack of independent reading in students' lives. We know students need to read text closely, understand its many aspects, analyze it, and respond competently and reasonably. They need to be informed citizens—critical readers and thinkers.

A hefty portion of our response stems from the four questions of close and critical reading and the college and career readiness standards. We have also used the Cognitive Rigor Matrix developed by Karen K. Hess to keep our attention focused on rigor.

On the way to core meaning we used many strategies. In each, we supplied texts from the public domain and activities. Our sample answers represent our sincere attempts to provide you assistance with the demands of planning instruction in an increasingly hectic world. We do not intend these samples to be "the" answers, as the best thinking in your classroom will come from you and your students. We wish you good luck on your journey to the core!

Chapter Seven Works Cited

Baer, Justin D., Mark A. Kutner, and John P. Sabatini. *Basic Reading Skills and the Literacy of America's Least Literate Adults: Results From the 2003 National Assessment of Adult Literacy (NAAL) Supplemental Studies.* Washington, D.C.: National Center for Education Statistics, Institute of Education Sciences, U.S. Dept. of Education, 2009.

Bradshaw, Tom, Bonnie Nichols, and Mark Bauerlein. *Reading at Risk: A Survey of Literary Reading in America.* Rep. no. 46. Washington, D.C.: National Endowment for the Arts, 2004. June 2004. Web. 15 July 2013.

Constitution of the United States—Official. U.S. Government National Archives and Records Administration. n.d. Web. 15 July 2013.

Declaration of Independence. U.S. Government National Archives and Records Administration. n.d. Web. 15 July 2013.

HCM Strategists. *The American Dream Report 2.0: How Financial Aid Can Help Improve College Access, Affordability, and Completion."* HCM Strategists. n.d. Web. 16 July 2013.

Jefferson, Thomas. "Letter to James Madison: December 20, 1787." *Teaching American History.org.* Ashland University Ashbrook Center. 2006–12. Web. 27 August 2013.

Jefferson, Thomas. "University of Virginia Library *Digital Curation Services.*" Digital Curation Services. University of Virginia Library, n.d. Web. 18 July 2013.

Kittle, Penny. *Penny Kittle Videos: Reading 2011.* Penny Kittle, n.d. Web. 16 July 2013.

Lehr, C. A., Johnson, D. R., Bremer, C. D., Cosio, A., & Thompson, M. *Essential tools: Increasing rates of school completion: Moving from policy and research to practice.* Minneapolis, MN: University of Minnesota, Institute on Community Integration, National Center on Secondary Education and Transition, 2004.

Mehegan, David. "Young People Reading a Lot Less." Boston Globe. 19 November 2007. *Boston. com.* Web. 17 July 2013.

National Commission on Adult Literacy. *National Assessment of Adult Literacy 2003.* In National Center for Family Literacy. "Statistics." n.d. Web. 16 July 2013.

------------. *Reach Higher, America: Overcoming Crisis in the U.S Workforce.* June 2008. Web. 16 July 2013.

National Governors Association Center for Best Practices, Council of Chief State School Officers. "Read the Common Core Standards." *Common Core State Standards Initiative.* National Governors Association Center for Best Practices, Council of Chief State School Officers, Washington, D.C., 2010. Web. 15 July 2013.

Paige, David D., Timothy V. Rasinski, and Theresa Magpuri-Lavell. "Is Fluent, Expressive Reading Important for High School Readers?" *Journal of Adolescent & Adult Literacy:* V56 n1 pp. 67–71 September 2012.

Pledge of Allegiance. United States District Court Southern District of West Virginia, n.d. Web. 15 July 2013.

"Primary Documents in American History." *Articles of Confederation: Primary Documents of American History.* Virtual Programs & Services. Library of Congress, n.d. Web. 15 July 2013.

Rasinski et al. "Reading Fluency." *Handbook of Reading Research.* Vol. 4. New York: Routledge, 2011.

Reagan, Ronald. "Inaugural Address 1967." *Ronald Reagan Presidential Library, National Archives and Records Administration.* Ronald Reagan Presidential Library, n.d. Web. 17 July 2013.

Roosevelt, Franklin D. "More Important Than God": FDR's First Fireside Chat. Franklin D. Roosevelt Library, n.d. Web. 16 July 2013.

Senge, Peter M. *The Fifth Discipline: The Art and Practice of the Learning Organization.* New York: Doubleday/Currency, 1990. Print.

U.S. Department of Education National Center for Educational Statistics. *NAEP 2009 Year in Review.* National Assessment of Educational Progress. n.d. Web. 15 July 2013.

U.S. Congress, Office of Technology Assessment. "Testing in American Schools; Asking the Right Questions." *Http://ota-cdn.fas.org/reports/9236.pdf.* Washington, D.C.: U.S. Government Printing Office, n.d. Web.

APPENDIX: **LIST OF APPENDICES**

Appendix 1a: Close and Critical Reading Questions Bookmarks

Close and Critical Reading Question #1 Restatement	Close and Critical Reading Question #2 Description	Close and Critical Reading Question #3 Interpretation	Close and Critical Reading Question #4 Application
What does the text say?	**How does the text say it?**	**What does the text mean?**	**So, what?**
Write a shortened version of the text containing only the main points and logical inferences. • How would you summarize or write a shortened version of the text containing only the main points? *CC1, CC2* • What is the gist/central idea? *CC1, CC2* • What is the specific textual evidence used to support the central idea? *CC1* • What are the most important ideas/events? *CC1, CC2* • What are the ideas in order of importance or presentation? *CC1* • What ideas might the author be suggesting rather than directly stating? What can you infer (obvious, logical inferences) from these hints or suggestions? *CC1*	**What techniques of craft and structure does the author use in the text? What are the genre, organization, features, word choice, figures of speech, etc.?** • How is the information organized (e.g., time, topic, argument, chapter, scene, stanza, etc.)? *CC5* • What genre does the selection represent? *CC5* • How does the piece open—exposition, lead, etc.? *CC5* • Whose voice did the author choose as narrator? *CC3* • From what point of view was this written? *CC3* • What are the sources of information and fact? Is there more than one source of information? *CC3* • What role does dialogue play in the text? *CC3* • What kind of language is used—dialect, variant spellings, archaic words, etc.? *CC4* • What are the style, mood, and tone? *CC4* • What word choice, imagery, and figures of speech (e.g., simile, metaphor, alliteration, irony, repetition, personification, etc.) does the author use? *CC4* • What diction and sentence structure does the author use, and how do the sections of the text relate to each other—from the sentence and paragraph levels to the section and chapter levels? *CC4*	**What is the theme/thesis of the text and how do the author's choice of content, structure, and craft combine to achieve his/her purpose?** • What is the central idea/thesis/theme of the text? *CC2* • How does the author support the central idea, thesis, or theme with ideas and details? *CC2* • What are the purposes, ends, and objectives? *CC2* • What is the author's stance/ perspective towards the topic? *CC6* • How does the author use language: dialect, variant spellings, archaic words, formal or informal words, etc., to shape the tone (the author's attitude toward the subject) and the meaning of the piece? *CC6* • How does the author use point of view, style, mood, tone, text features, imagery, figures of speech (e.g., simile, metaphor, alliteration, irony, repetition, onomatopoeia, personification, etc.) and the lead, etc., to achieve his/her purpose (author's intent)? *CC6* • Why does the author choose the method of presentation? *CC8* • What are the concepts that make the reasoning possible, what assumptions underlie the concepts, and what implications follow from the concepts? *CC7, CC8* • What does the author want the reader to believe? *CC7, CC8* • What is the quality of information collected; are the sources sufficient, relevant, credible, current? *CC7, CC8* • Who or what is not represented? Why? *CC7, CC8*	**Evaluation and integration: What does the theme/thesis mean in your life and/or in the lives of others—text-to-self, text-to-text, and/or text-to-world?** **Text(s)-to-self:** *CC7* • What does this remind me of in my life? • What is this similar to in my life? • How is this different from my life? • Has something like this ever happened to me? • How does this relate to my life? • What were my feelings when I read this? **Text(s)-to-text:** *CC9* • What does this remind me of in another book I've read? • How is this text similar to other things I've read? • How is this different from other books I've read? • Have I read about something like this before? **Text(s)-to-world:** *CC7* • What does this remind me of in the real world? • How is this text similar to things that happen in the real world? • How does this differ from things that happen in the real world? • How did that part relate to the world around me?

CC designations refer to standards from Common Core College and Career Readiness Anchor Standards for Reading.
From *Guided Highlighted Reading* by Weber, Schofield, and Nelson (Maupin House, 2012)

Appendix 2a: Summary Rubric—Common Core Reading Anchor Standards

CC Reading Anchor Standards	3 Complete	2 Partial	1 Minimal	Score
1. Read closely to determine what the text says explicitly and to make logical inferences from it; cite specific textual evidence when writing or speaking to support conclusions drawn from the text.	Reading Anchor # 1 Response: • states what the text says explicitly. (3 points) • makes logical inferences and cites specific textual evidence to support conclusions drawn from the text. (3 points)	Reading Anchor #1 Response: • includes much of what the text says explicitly. (2 points) • makes some logical inferences and cites general textual evidence to support some of the conclusions drawn from the text. (2 points)	Reading Anchor #1 Response: • includes little of what the text says explicitly. (1 point) • makes few logical inferences and gives little support drawn from the text. (1 point)	**__/6 pts.**
2. Determine central ideas or themes of a text and analyze their development; summarize the key supporting details and ideas.	Reading Anchor #2 Response: • summarizes using clearly identified central or main ideas. (3 points) • supports central ideas well with key details and ideas from the text. (3 points)	Reading Anchor #2 Response: • summarizes using partially or ineffectively identified central or main ideas. (2 points) • supports central ideas with some details and ideas from the text. (2 points)	Reading Anchor #2 Response: • summarizes using inaccurately identified central or main ideas. (1 point) • supports central ideas with few details and ideas from the text. (1 point)	**__/6 pts.**
3. Analyze how and why individuals, events, and ideas develop and interact over the course of a text.	Reading Anchor #3 Response expertly analyzes in detail where, when, why, and how events, ideas, and characters develop and interact. (Literature) (3 points)	Reading Anchor #3 Response partially analyzes in detail where, when, why, and how events, ideas, and characters develop and interact. (Literature) (2 points)	Reading Anchor #3 Response analyzes with little detail where, when, why, and how events, ideas, and characters develop and interact. (Literature) (1 point)	**__/3pts.** **Total** **__/15pts.**

From *Guided Highlighted Reading* by Weber, Schofield, and Nelson (Maupin House, 2012)

Appendix 3a: Craft and Structure Mining Maps

Mining Informational Text for Author's Craft: "How Does the Author Say It?"

TEXT STRUCTURE				
Genre	**Organization**	**Point of View/ Perspective**	**Tone/Mood**	**Text Features**
• Essay • Article—Internet, magazine, news, feature, editorial/op ed • Report • Research Report • Scholarly Article • Pamphlet • Journal/Diary/Letter • Memoir/ Autobiography/ Biography • Documentary • Speech	• Thesis/Claim with Support • Comparison/ Contrast • Cause & Effect • Problem & Solution • Description/ Definition • Enumeration • Chronology/ Sequence/ Procedure • Directions/How-to • Explanation • Question/Answer • Hierarchy	**Points of View:** • First Person • Second Person • Third Person **Narrator's Perspective:** • Ancient/ Modern/ Futuristic Time (check date of publication) • Naïve/Sophisticated Narrator • Expert/Novice • Reliable/Unreliable Narrator • Involved (firsthand)/ Uninvolved (secondhand) Narrator • Subjective/Objective Narrator	**Tone** • Informal/ Conversational • Formal/Academic/ Scholarly • Serious/ Straightforward • Humorous/Playful • Disdainful/ Condescending • Pessimistic/Optimistic • Biased/Objective	• Title/Title Page • Publication Information (publisher, city, date) • Table of Contents/ Index • Foreword/Preface/ Dedication • Illustrations/Pictures/ • Graphics/Diagrams • Captions • Headings/Subheadings • Margin Notes/Pullouts • Maps/Charts • Footnotes • Appendix • Glossary • Bibliography • Print Features (font, font size, color, white space)

AUTHOR'S CRAFT	
Terms	**Writing Techniques**
• Simile • Metaphor/Extended Metaphor • Personification • Symbolism • Exaggeration/Hyperbole • Allusion • Satire/Parody • Irony/Sarcasm • Over-/Understatement • Oxymoron • Repetition/Omission • Contrast **Sound** • Alliteration • Onomatopoeia • Assonance/Consonance • Euphony/Cacophony	• Lead • Show—Not Tell • Statistics • Professional Vocabulary/Domain-specific Nomenclature • Technical Vocabulary • Language/Word Choice—precise, scholarly, scientific, literary • Citation of Experts—books, articles, journals, speeches, research reports • Precise/Detailed Examples • Examples with Audience Appeal/Interest • Variation in Sentence Length and Format • Punctuation for Effect—ellipses, parentheses, exclamation points, boldface, italics

Appendix 3a: Craft and Structure Mining Maps

Mining Informational Text for Author's Craft: "How Does the Author Say It?"

Genre (Specific)	Organization	Tone/Mood	Point of View
• Short Story • Novel • Novella • Realistic Fiction (adventure, mystery) • Science Fiction • Historical Fiction • Fantasy/Fairy Tales • Myth • Legend • Tall Tale • Epic • Fable • Parable/Proverb • Pour Quoi Tale • Journal/Diary • Essay • Allegory • Drama	• Comparison/Contrast • Cause/Effect • Description/Enumeration • Problem/Solution • Chronology • Story/Play within Story/Play • Time Shifts—flashback, foreshadowing, time travel • Story Elements – characters – setting (geographic, temporal, social) – conflict (man vs. man, man vs. nature/supernatural, man vs. society, man vs. self, man vs. fate) – exposition – rising/falling action – climax – resolution	• Formal/Informal • Satiric • Humorous • Mournful • Frivolous • Mysterious • Dark • Romantic • Pessimistic/Optimistic • Childlike/Childish • Biased	• First Person • Third Person • Omniscient • Limited Omniscient

Text Features	Imagery/Figures of Speech	Writing Techniques
• Print Features—font, font size, color, white space, layout • Title • Chapters/Table of Contents • Illustrations **Poetry** • Verse—rhymed, free, blank • Meter/Rhythm • Scan—foot, iamb, trochee, dactyl • Rhyme/Rhyme Scheme • Form—sonnet, epic, ballad, elegy, Haiku, limerick, ode • Stanzas—couplet, triplet, quatrain **Drama** • Protagonist/Antagonist • Acts, Scenes • Dialogue/Monologue/Soliloquy/Aside • Stage Directions	• Simile • Metaphor/Extended Metaphor • Personification • Allusion • Apostrophe • Satire/Parody • Exaggeration/Hyperbole • Irony/Sarcasm/Oxymoron/Paradox • Repetition/Omission • Symbolism • Over-/Understatement • Vivid Description	• Word Choice/Language—precise, poetic, literary, period • Detail vs. "glowing generalities" • Character/Plot Development in Dialogue—soliloquy, aside, internal dialogue • Strong Lead—question, humor • Variation in Sentence Length • Suspense/Curiosity/Surprise • Motif • Sound Devices—alliteration, assonance, consonance, onomatopoeia, euphony, cacophony, • Punctuation for Effect—ellipses, parentheses, exclamation points, boldface, italics

Chapter 3 Appendix 3b: Author's Craft Game Cards

Author's Craft Game
Figures of Speech/Sound Devices

Teacher Directions

Give each group of students the cards in Appendix 3b, and give a copy of the same informational text to each student in the group. At the beginning of the year/semester, you might provide copies of a text with figurative language examples underlined as a scaffolding support. As students become more familiar with the terms, the underlining should no longer be necessary.

A student draws a card and looks for an example of the term in the text provided or creates one in an appropriate place in the text. After an allotted amount of time, the teacher identifies the examples and students check their work. Discuss any examples that students find that were not ones the teacher identified.

Author's Craft Game
Figures of Speech/Sound Devices

Directions

Students work in small groups (4–6 students) facing one another. Each student has a copy of the same short piece of informational text, and each group has one set of the cards.

The cards are placed facedown in the center of the table. Students take turns drawing a card.

When they have drawn a card, students read the directions to the group. They play the game by responding to the card by either finding the figure of speech (1 point) or creating one in an appropriate place in the text (2 points).

If they cannot respond in either way, the card is put faceup on the table, and the next player can either draw a card from the pile or take the discarded card and play it. Play continues until all cards are played. Scores are tallied to determine the winner.

Author's Craft
Figures of Speech/Sound Devices

Can you find a RHETORICAL QUESTION?

A **rhetorical question** is one the author asks without expecting an answer—simply for the impact it will have on the reader.

Examples:
- **Do you agree with me on this?**
- **Will we eliminate poverty?**
- **Do you hear me?**

Author's Craft
Figures of Speech/Sound Devices

Can you find a SIMILE or a METAPHOR?

A **simile** compares two things that are different, yet have some essential similarity, using *like* or *as*. A **metaphor** compares them directly, without using *like* or *as*.

Examples:
- **Simile: He acts like a clown.**
- **Metaphor: Her eyes are sapphires.**
- **Simile: She is like a feather in the breeze.**
- **Metaphor: Running, he was the wind. Sitting, he was a live wire.**

Author's Craft
Figures of Speech/Sound Devices

Can you find PERSONIFICATION?

Personification gives human characteristics to things that are not human, e.g., inanimate objects.

Examples:
- **Flowers turned their faces to thank the sun.**
- **Dandelion seeds danced in the breeze.**
- **The washing machine ate its way through the pile of laundry.**

Author's Craft
Figures of Speech/Sound Devices

Can you find ALLITERATION?

Alliteration is a pattern of repeated beginning sounds in words close together.

Examples:
- **Can you bear the burden of boredom?**
- **The long length of licorice lured the child.**
- **Fear false friends.**

Author's Craft
Figures of Speech/Sound Devices

Can you find REPETITION?

Repetition is the repeating of elements in writing—usually words but also sounds, letters, or phrase/sentence formats.

Examples:
- **How much wood could a woodchuck chuck if a woodchuck could chuck wood?**
- **Fear not the day, and fear not the light. Fear only the sharp edge of night.**
- **Draw courage from your love, for your love draws courage from you.**

Author's Craft
Figures of Speech/Sound Devices

Can you find HYPERBOLE?

Hyperbole is exaggeration for effect.

Examples:
- **I have a million things to do.**
- **The fall gave her a knot on her head the size of a softball.**
- **Her tears formed a river that carried her away.**

Author's Craft
Figures of Speech/Sound Devices

Can you find an ALLUSION?

An **allusion** is a reference to something from history or literature.

Examples:
- **People spoke in different languages, making the room a regular Tower of Babel.**
- **When he began his speech with "Four score and seven years ago," we could tell he had read Lincoln's Gettysburg Address.**

Author's Craft
Figures of Speech/Sound Devices

Can you find IRONY?

Irony is a conflict between reality and appearance or between what someone says and what he/she means.

Examples:
- **John sold his camera to buy his wife a program for her computer. She sold her computer to buy him a lens for his camera.**
- **Just as we finished recreating the lost document, we found the original.**
- **"Well, you're certainly concerned about tardiness today," said to a person who's two hours late. (verbal irony)**

Author's Craft
Figures of Speech/Sound Devices

Can you find an OXYMORON?

Oxymoron is a very briefly stated (often two words) contradictory statement.

Examples:
- **She was a delightful nuisance.**
- **He was an all-seeing sightless man.**
- **"O loving hate!" (Shakespeare)**

Author's Craft
Figures of Speech/Sound Devices

Can you find ONOMATOPOEIA?

Onomatopoeia refers to words whose sound suggests their meaning.

Examples:
- **We remained silent for hours, and then the loud bang of a locker door signaled an end to quiet time.**
- **The buzz of the mosquitoes was incessant.**
- **Is the hiss of this incessant whispering necessary?**

Author's Craft
Figures of Speech/Sound Devices

Can you find a SYMBOL?

A **symbol** is a word or expression that represents an idea.

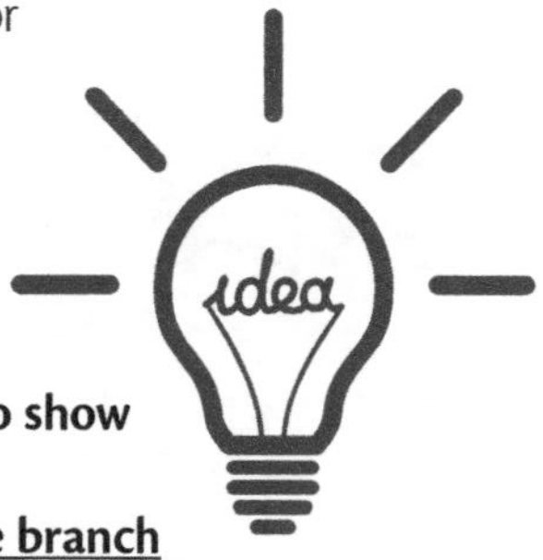

Examples:
- **He carried a flag to show his patriotism.**
- **The dove and olive branch have come to represent peace.**
- **The lamp of learning glowed for me once I learned to read.**

Author's Craft
Figures of Speech/Sound Devices

Can you find an UNDERSTATEMENT?

Understatement is saying less than is true.

Examples:
- **He closed the door on the sub-zero weather and said, "It's chilly out there."**
- **He described the seven-foot-tall man as "on the tall side."**

Author's Craft

Figures of Speech/Sound Devices

Can you find a PARADOX?

Paradox is a statement that appears to contradict itself yet it is true.

Examples:

- **The game was lively, engaging, and mentally challenging—exactly what we had requested. We hated it.**
- **We must turn left in order to go right.**

Author's Craft

Figures of Speech/Sound Devices

Can you find a RHYME?

Rhyme involves identical or close ending sounds in two or more words, either at the ends of lines of poetry or near each other in a text.

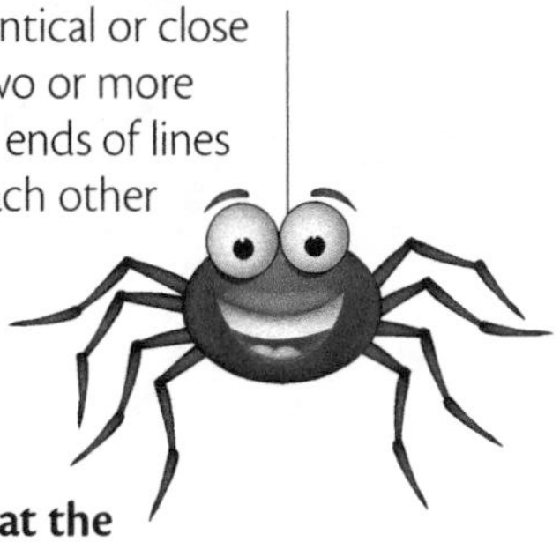

Examples:

- **The fountain lay at the foot of the mountain.**
- **We were about to dine**
  When the spider ran up her spine.
  Alas, our evening was no longer fine.

Author's Craft

Figures of Speech/Sound Devices

Can you find CONTRAST?

Contrast places opposing ideas next to or near each other in a way that encourages consideration.

Examples:

- **We should be stronger, not weaker.**
- **The winners will be honored, not shunned.**
- **Good people sought to help; evil people wished to harm.**

Author's Craft

Figures of Speech/Sound Devices

Can you find ASSONANCE?

Assonance is repetition of vowel sounds within words.

Examples:

- **How will the town turn around?**
- **I will buy the boat before high tide. (This could also be an example of alliteration: buy, boat, before.)**
- **The trees feel the breeze.**

Author's Craft

Figures of Speech/Sound Devices

Can you find CONSONANCE?

Consonance is repetition of consonant sounds appearing within words or preceded by different vowel sounds at the ends of words.

Examples:

- **The hissing of the asp pesters me so! (Hissing could also be an example of onomatopoeia.)**
- **When the time comes, it may not seem right.**

Author's Craft

Figures of Speech/Sound Devices

Can you find EUPHONY/CACOPHONY?

Euphony is pleasant combinations of sounds. **Cacophony** is unpleasant combinations of sounds.

Examples:

- **E: The song of the South simmered on steamy mornings.**
- **C: My cold, hacking cough caught the buzzard's attention.**
- **E: The mellow murmuring lulls us to sleep.**
- **C: The rat-tat-tat of the gun grew bolder, demanding attention.**

Appendix 3c: GHR for Craft—Kennedy Inaugural Questions

Guided Highlighted Reading for Craft
John F. Kennedy's Inaugural Address Excerpt—Conclusion Text

In your hands, my fellow citizens, more than mine, will rest the final success or failure of our course. Since this country was founded, each generation of Americans has been summoned to give testimony to its national loyalty. The graves of young Americans who answered the call to service surround the globe.

Now the trumpet summons us again—not as a call to bear arms, though arms we need—not as a call to battle, though embattled we are—but a call to bear the burden of a long twilight struggle, year in and year out, "rejoicing in hope, patient in tribulation"—a struggle against the common enemies of man: tyranny, poverty, disease and war itself.

Can we forge against these enemies a grand and global alliance, North and South, East and West, that can assure a more fruitful life for all mankind? Will you join in that historic effort?

In the long history of the world, only a few generations have been granted the role of defending freedom in its hour of maximum danger. I do not shrink from this responsibility—I welcome it. I do not believe that any of us would exchange places with any other people or any other generation. The energy, the faith, the devotion which we bring to this endeavor will light our country and all who serve it—and the glow from that fire can truly light the world.

And so, my fellow Americans: ask not what your country can do for you—ask what you can do for your country.

My fellow citizens of the world: ask not what America will do for you, but what together we can do for the freedom of man.

Finally, whether you are citizens of America or citizens of the world, ask of us here the same high standards of strength and sacrifice which we ask of you. With a good conscience our only sure reward, with history the final judge of our deeds, let us go forth to lead the land we love, asking His blessing and His help, but knowing that here on earth God's work must truly be our own.

Approximate Lexile Level: 1220

Guided Highlighted Reading for Craft
John F. Kennedy's Inaugural Address Excerpt—Conclusion
Questions

Directions: Read the following prompts while students highlight as directed.

1. In line 1, highlight the phrase in which Kennedy addresses his listeners in second person ("you"/"your") to focus directly on them and to increase their sense of involvement in the course ahead. ("in **your** hands")

2. In lines 1-2, highlight the first-person pronouns ("I"/"me"/ "my"/ "mine," "we"/ "us"/ "our"/ "ours") that indicate Kennedy's personal involvement in the course ahead. ("my," "mine," "our")

3. Authors use concrete objects to represent or symbolize other things or even concepts. In line 3, highlight the word that symbolizes the soldiers who have died while serving America. ("graves")

4. In line 4, highlight the words that serve as a more poetic way of saying "served their country." ("answered the call to service")
5. A metaphor directly compares two things that are different yet have some essential similarity. In line 5, highlight the words that serve as a metaphor for a call for help. ("the trumpet summons us again")
6. Parallelism is when an author repeats words and phrasing for ideas that are of similar type and importance. In lines 5–6, highlight the sections that are parallel. ("…not as a call to bear arms, though arms we need—not as a call to battle, though embattled we are….")
7. A metaphor directly compares two things that are different yet have some essential similarity. In lines 6–7, highlight the words that serve as a metaphor for the work that lies ahead. ("a long twilight struggle")
8. An allusion is a reference to an event, object, or figure from literature or history. In line 7, highlight the quoted words that come from the Bible. ("rejoicing in hope, patient in tribulation")
9. Alliteration is a pattern of repeated beginning sounds in words close together. In line 9, highlight the words that have the same beginning sound and are examples of alliteration. ("**g**rand and **g**lobal")
10. A rhetorical question is a question that the speaker or writer asks for the effect it has but does not expect an answer. Highlight the rhetorical question in lines 10–11. ("Will you join in that historic effort?")
11. In lines 13–15, highlight the words that use first person ("I"/"me"/ "my"/ "mine," "we"/ "us"/ "our"/ "ours") to demonstrate to the audience that Kennedy wanted to join the defense of freedom. ("**I** do not shrink from this responsibility—**I** welcome it. **I** do not believe that any of **us** would exchange places with any other people or any other generation.")
12. A metaphor directly compares two things that are different yet have some essential similarity. In lines 16–17, highlight the words that serve as metaphors to represent what Americans will bring to the defense of freedom. ("…will light our country and all who serve it—and the glow from that fire can truly light the world.") *Energy, faith, and devotion are what they will actually bring. The metaphors for those are the "fire" and accompanying "light" and "glow."*
13. Kennedy was known for an inverted repetition called *chiasmus*. Highlight the two sections of the sentence in lines 18–19 that are parallel in structure but in reverse order. ("what your country can do for you" and "what you can do for your country")
14. In line 20, highlight the words that Kennedy used to broaden his perspective from America to all people on Earth. ("my fellow citizens of the world")
15. Alliteration is a pattern of repeated beginning sounds in words close together. Highlight the alliteration in line 23. ("**s**tandards of **s**trength and **s**acrifice")
16. Alliteration is a pattern of repeated beginning sounds in words close together. Highlight the phrase in line 25 that includes alliteration. ("to **l**ead the **l**and we **l**ove")

Appendix 3d: GHR Hoover Questions

Guided Highlighted Reading
Herbert Hoover Inaugural Address Excerpt
Monday, March 4, 1929

WORLD PEACE

The United States fully accepts the profound truth that our own progress, prosperity, and peace are interlocked with the progress, prosperity, and peace of all humanity. The whole world is at peace. The dangers to a continuation of this peace to-day are largely the fear and suspicion which still haunt the world. No suspicion or fear can be rightly directed toward our country.

Those who have a true understanding of America know that we have no desire for territorial expansion, for economic or other domination of other peoples. Such purposes are repugnant to our ideals of human freedom. Our form of government is ill adapted to the responsibilities which inevitably follow permanent limitation of the independence of other peoples. Superficial observers seem to find no destiny for our abounding increase in population, in wealth and power except that of imperialism. They fail to see that the American people are engrossed in the building for themselves of a new economic system, a new social system, a new political system all of which are characterized by aspirations of freedom of opportunity and thereby are the negation of imperialism. They fail to realize that because of our abounding prosperity our youth are pressing more and more into our institutions of learning; that our people are seeking a larger vision through art, literature, science, and travel; that they are moving toward stronger moral and spiritual life--that from these things our sympathies are broadening beyond the bounds of our Nation and race toward their true expression in a real brotherhood of man. They fail to see that the idealism of America will lead it to no narrow or selfish channel, but inspire it to do its full share as a nation toward the advancement of civilization. It will do that not by mere declaration but by taking a practical part in supporting all useful international undertakings. We not only desire peace with the world, but to see peace maintained throughout the world. We wish to advance the reign of justice and reason toward the extinction of force.

The recent treaty for the renunciation of war as an instrument of national policy sets an advanced standard in our conception of the relations of nations. Its acceptance should pave the way to greater limitation of armament, the offer of which we sincerely extend to the world. But its full realization also implies a greater and greater perfection in the instrumentalities for pacific settlement of controversies between nations. In the creation and use of these instrumentalities we should support every sound method of conciliation, arbitration, and judicial settlement. American statesmen were among the first to propose and they have constantly urged upon the world, the establishment of a tribunal for the settlement of controversies of a justiciable character. The Permanent Court of International Justice in its major purpose is thus peculiarly identified with American ideals and with American statesmanship. No more potent instrumentality for this purpose has ever been conceived and no other is practicable of establishment. The reservations placed upon our adherence should not be misinterpreted. The United States seeks by these reservations no special privilege or advantage but only to clarify our relation to advisory opinions and other matters which are subsidiary to the major purpose of the court. The way should, and I believe will, be found by which we may take our proper place in a movement so fundamental to the progress of peace.

Appendix 3d: GHR Hoover Questions

Our people have determined that we should make no political engagements such as membership in the League of Nations, which may commit us in advance as a nation to become involved in the settlements of controversies between other countries. They adhere to the belief that the independence of America from such obligations increases its ability and availability for service in all fields of human progress.

I have lately returned from a journey among our sister Republics of the Western Hemisphere. I have received unbounded hospitality and courtesy as their expression of friendliness to our country. We are held by particular bonds of sympathy and common interest with them. They are each of them building a racial character and a culture which is an impressive contribution to human progress. We wish only for the maintenance of their independence, the growth of their stability, and their prosperity. While we have had wars in the Western Hemisphere, yet on the whole the record is in encouraging contrast with that of other parts of the world. Fortunately the New World is largely free from the inheritances of fear and distrust which have so troubled the Old World. We should keep it so.

It is impossible, my countrymen, to speak of peace without profound emotion. In thousands of homes in America, in millions of homes around the world, there are vacant chairs. It would be a shameful confession of our unworthiness if it should develop that we have abandoned the hope for which all these men died. Surely civilization is old enough, surely mankind is mature enough so that we ought in our own lifetime to find a way to permanent peace. Abroad, to west and east, are nations whose sons mingled their blood with the blood of our sons on the battlefields. Most of these nations have contributed to our race, to our culture, our knowledge, and our progress. From one of them we derive our very language and from many of them much of the genius of our institutions. Their desire for peace is as deep and sincere as our own.

Peace can be contributed to by respect for our ability in defense. Peace can be promoted by the limitation of arms and by the creation of the instrumentalities for peaceful settlement of controversies. But it will become a reality only through self-restraint and active effort in friendliness and helpfulness. I covet for this administration a record of having further contributed to advance the cause of peace.

Each student will need highlighters in two different colors. Divide the questions into two sections, reading first the odd-numbered questions, asking students to highlight in one color, and then reading the even-numbered questions with the students using another color highlighter.

Guided Highlighted Reading Herbert Hoover Inaugural Address Excerpt Craft Questions

1. Alliteration is a pattern of repeated beginning sounds in words close together. In lines 6–7, highlight the words that are examples of alliteration. ("**p**rofound," "**p**rogress, **p**rosperity," "**p**eace," "**p**rogress, **p**rosperity," "**p**eace")
2. Highlight the sentence in lines 7–8 that Hoover may have intended to provide a sense of comfort or stability. ("The whole world is at peace.")
3. In line 9, highlight the words that may suggest concern or discomfort. ("suspicion," "haunt," "suspicion," "fear")
4. In line 12, highlight the group of words that identifies the people who know that America has no desire for territorial expansion or any domination of other peoples. ("Those who have a true understanding of America")
5. In line 14, highlight the word that carries the idea of something offensive or unacceptable. ("repugnant")
6. Highlight the words in line 16 that identify those who think America's only destiny is imperialism. ("superficial observers")
7. In lines 18–19, highlight the words that name the things Hoover said are "the negation of imperialism." ("a new economic system, a new social system, a new political system")
8. In line 21, highlight the words that provide the reason more young people are seeking higher education; people are appreciating art, literature, science, and travel; and people are leading stronger moral and spiritual lives. ("because of our abounding prosperity")
9. Alliteration is a pattern of repeated beginning sounds in words close together. In line 24, highlight the words that are an example of alliteration. ("**b**roadening **b**eyond the **b**ounds" or possibly "**th**at ... **th**ese **th**ings")
10. In line 25, highlight the words that suggest Hoover saw genuine hope for building bonds with other peoples. ("a real brotherhood of man")
11. Highlight the words in lines 28–29 that tell how America will work toward the advancement of civilization. ("by taking a practical part in supporting all useful international undertakings")
12. When something is extinct, it no longer exists. In line 30, highlight the words that tell what type of action Hoover wanted to take to make force extinct. ("advance the reign of justice and reason")
13. In line 34, highlight the words that repeat ending sounds to make a form of rhyme. ("relations of nations")

14. Highlight in line 35 the words that mean "reduction in the number of weapons." ("limitation of armament")

15. In line 37, highlight the words that mean "peaceful solution of disagreements." ("pacific settlement of controversies")

16. Highlight in lines 38–39 the words Hoover chose that suggest peaceful solutions to try first. ("conciliation, arbitration, and judicial settlement")

17. Repetition means the repeating of the same words or an arrangement of words. In lines 42–43, highlight the words that are an example of repetition. ("with American ideals and with American statesmanship")

18. Highlight in line 47 the word that suggests something is of lesser significance or importance. ("subsidiary")

19. Alliteration is a pattern of repeated beginning sounds in words close together. In lines 48–49, highlight the words that are examples of alliteration. ("**p**roper **p**lace" and "**p**rogress of **p**eace")

20. In line 51, highlight the words that Hoover most likely intended to suggest a warmth and unity among the citizens listening to him. ("our people")

21. In line 57, highlight the words that suggest a warm family relationship with other countries. ("our sister Republics")

22. Highlight in line 58 the word that means "without limits." ("unbounded")

23. In line 59, highlight the words that identify troubles Hoover saw in the Old World. ("inheritances of fear and distrust")

24. A symbol is a word or expression that represents another thing or idea. Highlight the words in lines 69–70 that symbolize the people who died in war. ("vacant chairs")

25. Repetition means the repeating of the same words or an arrangement of words. Highlight the words in lines 71–72 that are an example of repetition of an arrangement of similar words within the sentence. ("surely civilization is old enough, surely mankind is mature enough")

26. Alliteration is a pattern of repeated beginning sounds in words close together. In line 73, what words are an example of alliteration? ("permanent peace")

27. In lines 73–74, highlight the words that suggest grief shared with other nations. ("...whose sons mingled their blood with the blood of our sons on the battlefields.")

28. In line 80, highlight the word that suggests that Hoover wants a plan for settling controversies. ("instrumentalities")

29. In lines 81–82, highlight the words that describe the important qualities of the work ahead. ("self-restraint," "active effort," friendliness," "helpfulness")

30. Highlight in line 82 the word that tells how badly Hoover wanted his presidency to have advanced peace. ("covet")

Appendix 4a: Mining Map for Political Cartoons

Mining the Potential of the Text: "How Does the Text Say It?"—Political Cartoon

TEXT STRUCTURE—Power to evoke laughter as well as humiliation; use of comedy to make readers think and draw connections/make a point

Genre	Organization	Point of View	Tone/Mood	Text Features
Editorial cartoon Political cartoon Humor cartoon Animated cartoon	Setting—geographical: local, state, national, international Setting—temporal Setting—social Single panel = cartoon Series of panels = text strip (comic strip)	Bird's-eye view—view from a high angle as if from a bird's vantage point Point of view of cartoonist Political viewpoint	Sarcastic Biting Cynical Satirical	Thought balloons Narration blocks Labels Captions Signs Layout and design: Border Gutters Open panel Panel Splash panel

AUTHOR'S CRAFT

Imagery/Figures of Speech via Visual	Cartoon Techniques
Symbols (for example, an elephant represents the Republican Party and a donkey represents the Democratic Party) Common symbol or image as metaphor Current events as visual metaphors Stereotypes Prejudices Allegory Opposing points of view Objects or characters as symbols Significant words or phrases Caricature that parodies the individual Allusion—indirect reference to past or current event which creates the situation or context into which the individual is placed Facial expressions Attire Body expression and appearance Recognizable event Color—symbolic meaning	Cynical—convey scorn or negativity or skepticism Satirical—use wit to convey insults Oversimplified opinions through stereotypes Caricature—exaggeration of personal characteristics to attack a particular person Satire—use of sarcasm or irony to make fun of somebody or of some event

Note: Author and Magazine Published in and date?

Appendix 4b.1: Website Evaluation Rubric for Grades 4–8

Scale	Authority and Currency	Purpose, Scope, and Depth of Content	Objectivity and Accuracy	Organization and Function of Presentation
Superior	Clearly provides all of the following: • author/organization • credentials/ qualifications • address (physical or email) and/or phone • reliable URL/ domain appropriate for content • notation of publication date or date of last revision	Contains extremely clear presentation of: • purpose • relevant information (no gaps or omissions) • integration of new information into topic area • a list of sources (bibliography)	Exceeds expectations for: • verifiable facts presented without bias • absence of errors (content, grammar, mechanics)	Contains exceptionally user-friendly and clear: • organization • menu or table of contents • vocabulary • active and logical links or connections between pages
Adequate	Somewhat clearly provides only the following: • author/organization • address (physical or email) • credible domain for content	Clearly presents: • purpose • relevant information (no gaps or omissions) • a list of sources (bibliography)	Meets the expectations for: • verifiable facts presented without bias • elimination of errors (content, grammar, mechanics)	Is helpful because it contains: • clear organization • understandable vocabulary • active links
Minimal	Tends to be somewhat confusing because it provides only author/ organization	Contains somewhat confusing and/ or incomplete presentation of: • purpose • relevant information (some gaps or omissions) • list of sources (bibliography)	Falls short of expectations but still contains: • verifiable facts presented without bias	Is somewhat difficult to use because it: • lacks clear organization • contains some very challenging vocabulary • has inactive links
Inadequate	May be obscure because it does not provide any of the following: • author/organization • credentials • address (physical or email) and/or phone	Has confusing presentation of: • purpose • relevant information (obvious gaps or omissions) • list of sources	Is troublesome because: • facts cannot be verified and/or • information is presented with bias	Is difficult to use because: • it lacks organization • vocabulary is challenging • links are not active

Appendix 4b.2: Website Evaluation Rubric for Grades 9–12

Scale	Authority and Currency	Purpose, Scope, and Depth of Content	Objectivity and Accuracy	Organization and Function of Presentation
Superior	Clearly provides all of the following: • author/organization • reliable credentials and/or affiliations • content that has been reviewed or verified or critiqued • publisher's address (physical or email) and/or phone number • active links to other reliable information • reliable URL/domain is appropriate for content • publication date or date of last revision	Very effectively presents: • a clear statement of purpose • clear indication of intent (popular, scholarly, satiric, serious) • relevant information (no gaps or omissions) • new information integrated into topic area • comprehensive vs. partial coverage or overview of topic • a list of sources/works cited (bibliography)	Exceeds expectations for: • presentation of verifiable facts without bias (If it presents a specific view, then it also presents opposing views fairly) • using language free of bias • avoiding errors (content, grammar, mechanics)	Provides exceptional help because it contains: • clear organization and focus • a menu or table of contents • understandable vocabulary • visual effects/icons that enhance but do not substitute for content • links to stable sites • links that are relevant, reliable, and appropriate • links that have been evaluated
Adequate	Somewhat clearly provides only the following: • author/organization • address (physical or email) • brief reference to affiliations • credible domain for content • current publication date and/or last update for user's topic	Presents relatively clear: • evidence of purpose • indication of intent (popular, scholarly, satiric, serious) • relevant information (no gaps or omissions) • list of sources (bibliography)	Meets the expectation for: • verifiable facts presented without bias (according to the intent of the site) • absence of errors (content, grammar, mechanics)	Provides useful assistance because it contains: • clear organization • understandable vocabulary • active links to stable sites • visual effects/icons appropriate for content
Minimal	Seems somewhat confusing because it provides only the following: • author/organization • outdated copyright and/or last update for user's topic	Contains somewhat confusing presentation of: • purpose • relevant information (some gaps or omissions) • incomplete list of sources (bibliography)	Falls short of expectations but still: • contains verifiable facts presented without bias (according to the intent of the site) • has few or no errors (content, grammar, mechanics)	Is challenging to use because it: • lacks clear organization • has either challenging or simplistic vocabulary • may substitute visual effects/icons for reliable content links
Inadequate	May be obscure because it does not provide any of the following: • author/organization • credentials • address (physical or email) and/or phone • date of copyright and/ or last update	Has confusing presentation of: • purpose • relevant information (obvious gaps or omissions) • inadequate list of sources (bibliography)	Presents information that: • cannot be verified • is presented with bias	Is of little use because it: • lacks organization • has challenging vocabulary • presents inactive or outdated links • contains visual effects/icons that are not appropriate for content

Appendix 4c: Reading Standard 7 Activity for Social Studies and History

An Activity for Reading Standard #7 for Literacy in History/Social Studies 6th–8th

Integrate visual information (e.g., in charts, graphs, photographs, videos, or maps) with other information in print and digital texts.

Quotations for Pre-reading

> "We define ourselves as a nation of immigrants. That's who we are—in our bones. The promise we see in those who come here from every corner of the globe, that's always been one of our greatest strengths." *–President Barack Obama*
>
> "Everywhere immigrants have enriched and strengthened the fabric of American life."
> *—John F. Kennedy*
>
> "Unless the stream of these people can be turned away from their country to other countries, they will soon outnumber us so that we will not be able to save our language or our government."
> *—Benjamin Franklin*

Find a dictionary definition of "immigrant" and put it in your own words. Then explore the interactive map from 1880–2000. Search for "New York Times Immigration Explorer." It should be one of the first choices in the list that results. Select an immigrant population and visually note the population's settlement across the United States through the decades.

ASSIGNMENT: Select a foreign-born group and an era on the interactive map. Find a website about the selected immigrant that you determine is valid, and use the Website Evaluation Rubric to determine the website's validity. Read more about the selected immigrant group and find a quotation that captures the American immigrant experience. Finally, select a photograph of an immigrant from the selected country and create a six-word story that captures the immigrant's experience.

Works Cited

Franklin, Benjamin. Quoted in "Four Quotes About Immigration." *Education World.* 2000. Web. 6 October 2013.

Kennedy, John. F. Quoted in "News Release: JFK Library To Host Naturalization Ceremony For More Than 200 New Citizens From 61 Different Countries." *Press Releases.* John F. Kennedy Presidential Library and Museum. 19 July 2006. 6 October 2013.

Obama, Barack. "Remarks by the President on Comprehensive Immigration Reform: Del Sol High School, Las Vegas, NV." *Speeches and Remarks.* The White House Office of Press Secretary. 29 January 2013. Web. 6 October 2013.

Appendix 4d: Mining Map for Photographs

<table>
<tr><th colspan="5">TEXT STRUCTURE: PHOTOGRAPHS</th></tr>
<tr><th>Genre (can blur or cross boundaries)</th><th>Composition</th><th>Point of View</th><th>Tone/Mood</th><th>Visual Elements</th></tr>
<tr>
<td rowspan="2">Photojournalism: Communicate news by photographs, which should be honest and impartial while telling the story. Contribute to news through 1) timeliness, 2) objectivity, 3) narration
Documentary Photography: Fact-based photographs of actual events and people. Can be a form of journalism or social commentary or propaganda or personal expression. Main purpose is to record a place, person(s), or event.
Abstract Photography
Aerial Photography
Architectural Photography
Astrophotography
Fashion Photography
Food Photography
Interior Design Photography
Landscape Photography
Long Exposure Photography
Macro Photography
Pet Photography
Photojournalism
Portrait Photography
Product Photography
Shot Exposure Photography (freezing time)
Sports Photography
Still Life Photography
Street Photography
Time Lapse Video
Underwater Photography
Weather Photography
Wedding Photography
Wildlife Photography</td>
<td rowspan="2">• Rule of thirds: Imagine breaking an image down into thirds (both horizontally and vertically) so that you have nine parts
• Rule of symmetry: Keep your subject symmetrical
• Asymmetry—lack of symmetry or an unevenness to create visual interest
• Background
• Balance—the distribution of the visual elements
• Setting—geographical, temporal, climatic, social
• Subject</td>
<td>• Bird's-eye view
• Angle (POV) includes front, behind, side, top, high, low, eye-level, tilted, neutral, etc.
• Angle—the vantage point</td>
<td>Capture or evoke emotion through:
• Lighting
• Colors
• Soft focus
• Filters
• Range of tone (What are the darkest and lightest values?)
• Subject expression</td>
<td>Focus (What appears sharpest in the photograph?)
• Light—are there shadows?
• Lines
• Shapes
• Repetition
• Space
• Texture</td>
</tr>
<tr>
<td>Imagery/ Figures of Speech
• metaphor
• motif
• symbol
• theme
• juxtaposed contrasting concepts
• allusion to previous texts</td>
<td colspan="2">Photographer's Techniques
• Long Shot (LS) or Full Shot (FS)
• Medium Shot (MS)
• Medium Close-up (MCU)
• Close-up (CU)
• Extreme Close-ups (XCUs)
Technical Concepts
• Shot types (long shot, close up, medium shot)
• Shot length
• Camera angles
• Lighting (backlighting)
• Color
• Framing
• Artistic eye and/or technical mastery
• Use of lighting and color
• Color combination
• Balance
• Details (people, objects, activities)
Unique Perspective
• Tell a story—capture history and/or freeze moment for others to witness (photojournalism does this best)
• Capture an iconic moment
• Leave something to the imagination</td>
</tr>
<tr><td colspan="2">Photographer:</td><td colspan="2">Publication:</td><td>Date of Publication:</td></tr>
</table>

4e: Close and Critical Reading for a Visual Text Rubric

Questions	3 (meets assignment)	2 (partially meets)	1 (minimally meets)	Score
What does the text say? (Briefly summarize the story.)	• Answer is accurate, significant, and relevant with many details and examples. • Details support point. • Word choice and conventions support meaning.	• Answer is accurate, significant, and relevant but has few details to support or explain the answer. • Attempts at organization are partially successful. • Word choice and errors in conventions do not distract from meaning.	• Answer is inaccurate or a misinterpretation with little or no relevance to text or question. • Ideas and content are not developed with details or appear random. • Word choice and errors in conventions may distract from meaning.	**Text #1** **____/3**
How does it say it? In other words, how does the artist develop the text to convey his/her purpose? (What are the genre, format, organization, features, materials, mediums, symbols, etc.?)	• Answer is relevant with many details and examples. • Details support point. • Word choice and conventions support meaning.	• Answer is relevant but has few details to support or explain the answer. • Attempts at organization are partially successful. • Word choice and errors in conventions do not distract from meaning.	• Answer contains misinterpretation and has little or no relevance to text, question, or genre. • Ideas and content are developed with few or no details. • Word choice and errors in conventions may distract from meaning.	**Text #1** **____/3**
What does the text mean? (What theme/ concept is the artist trying to get across?)	• Answer is relevant with many details and examples. • Details support point. • Word choice and conventions support meaning.	• Answer is relevant but has few details to support or explain the answer. • Attempts at organization are partially successful. • Word choice and errors in conventions do not distract from meaning.	• Answer contains misinterpretation and little or no relevance to text or question or is a retelling or summary. • Ideas are not devel-oped with details. • Word choice and errors in conventions may distract from meaning.	**Text #1** **____/3**
So what? (What does the message/theme/ concept mean in your life and/or in the lives of others? Why is it worth sharing/telling? What significance does it have to your life and/or to the lives of others?)	• Answer is relevant and/or insightful with many details and examples. • Details support point. • Word choice and conventions support meaning.	• Answer is relevant but has few details to support or explain the answer. • Attempts at organization are partially successful. • Word choice and errors in conventions do not distract from meaning.	• Answer contains misinterpretation and has little or no relevance to text or question. • Answer appears random or inappropriate. • Ideas and content are not developed with details. • Word choice and errors in conventions may distract from meaning.	**Text #1** **____/3** **TOTAL** **____/12**

From *Guided Highlighted Reading* by Weber, Schofield, and Nelson (Maupin House, 2012)

Appendix 4f: GHR Prompts for "The New Colossus"

"The New Colossus" by Emma Lazarus

1. Not like the brazen giant of Greek fame
2. With conquering limbs astride from land to land;
3. Here at our sea-washed, sunset gates shall stand
4. A mighty woman with a torch, whose flame
5. Is the imprisoned lightning, and her name
6. Mother of Exiles. From her beacon-hand
7. Glows world-wide welcome; her mild eyes command
8. The air-bridged harbor that twin cities frame.
9. "Keep, ancient lands, your storied pomp!" cries she
10. With silent lips. "Give me your tired, your poor,
11. Your huddled masses yearning to breathe free,
12. The wretched refuse of your teeming shore.
13. Send these, the homeless, tempest-tossed to me,
14. I lift my lamp beside the golden door!"

Guided Highlighted Reading for Content/Summary (Close and Critical Reading Question 1)

With a highlighter pen, follow the prompts of the teacher and highlight what the prompts instruct you to highlight.

The teacher reads the following:

Title: Find and highlight the title of the poem. *("The New Colossus")*

Line #1: Find and highlight what the new colossus is not like. ("brazen giant of Greek fame")

Line #4: Highlight the gender of the new colossus. ("woman")

Line #4: Highlight the adjective used to describe the colossus. ("mighty")

Line #6: Highlight the name of the new colossus. ("Mother of Exiles")

Lines #10–14: Highlight whom the new colossus desires. ("your tired, your poor,/Your huddled masses yearning to breathe free,/The wretched refuse,"/"homeless, tempest tossed")

Line #14: Highlight what the new colossus lifts to guide people to the door. ("lamp")

Guided Highlighted Reading for Craft, Structure, and Perspective (Close and Critical Reading Question 2)

With another copy of the passage or a different color highlighter pen, students highlight the following.

Title: Find and highlight the noun in the title of the poem. ("Colossus")

Sentence #1: Find and highlight the phrase that involves contrast. ("Not like")

Sentence #2: Find and highlight a phrase that implies immigration. ("land to land")

Sentence #3: Find and highlight the word that evokes the image of yellow or gold. ("sunset")

Sentence #3: Find and highlight the noun that provides entrance or exclusion. ("gates")

Sentence #4: Find and highlight a synonym for "strong/powerful." ("mighty")

Sentences #4 and #5: Find and highlight the two words that rhyme. ("flame," "name")

Sentence #6: Find and highlight the word that means "people who are cast out." ("Exiles")

Sentence #6: Find and highlight the noun that means "a guiding signal." ("beacon")

Sentence #9: Find and highlight the word that means "showiness or pageantry." ("pomp")

Sentence #10: Find and highlight the punctuation that indicates dialogue. (")

Sentence #11: Find and highlight the two-word phrase that evokes/creates a visual image in the reader's mind. ("huddled masses")

Sentence #12: Find and highlight the phrase that implies "disposable." ("wretched refuse")

Sentence #13: Find and highlight the alliteration. ("tempest-tossed")

Sentence #14: Find and highlight the word that is associated with wealth and riches. ("golden")

Appendix 5a: Roosevelt's Arbor Day Message

A Proclamation by
President Theodore Roosevelt, 1907:

To the School Children of the United States:

Arbor Day (which means simply "Tree Day") is now observed in every State in our Union—and mainly in the schools. At various times from January to December, but chiefly in this month of April, you give a day or part of a day to special exercises and perhaps to actual tree planting, in recognition of the importance of trees to us as a Nation, and of what they yield in adornment, comfort, and useful products to the communities in which you live.

It is well that you should celebrate your Arbor Day thoughtfully, for within your lifetime the Nation's need of trees will become serious. We of an older generation can get along without what we have, though with growing hardship; but in your full manhood and womanhood you will want what nature once so bountifully supplied, and man so thoughtlessly destroyed; and because of that want you will reproach us, not for what we have used, but for what we have wasted.

For the nation as for the man or woman and the boy or girl, the road to success is the right use of what we have and the improvement of present opportunity. If you neglect to prepare yourselves not for the duties and responsibilities which will fall upon you later, if you do not learn the things which you will need to know when your school days are over, you will suffer the consequences. So any nation which in its youth lives only for the day, reaps without sowing, and consumes without husbanding, must expect the penalty of the prodigal, whose labor could with difficulty find him the bare means of life.

Concluding Paragraph Informal Lexile Level: ll30L

A people without children would face a hopeless future; a country without trees is almost as hopeless; forests which are so used that they can not renew themselves will soon vanish, and with them all their benefits. A true forest is not merely a storehouse full of wood, but, as it were, a factory of wood, and at the same time a reservoir of water. When you help to preserve our forests or to plant new ones you are acting the part of good citizens. The value of forestry deserves, therefore, to be taught in the schools, which aim to make good citizens of you. If your Arbor Day exercises help you to realize what benefits each one of you receives from the forests, and how by your assistance these benefits may continue, they will serve a good end.

—*Theodore Roosevelt*

Roosevelt, Theodore. "A Proclamation by President Theodore Roosevelt, 1907: To the School Children of the United States." Arbor Day Foundation. n.d. Web. 19 May 2013.

Appendix 5b: CCSS Argument Sample—Pizza

Common Core State Standards with Progressing Text Commentary

The Common Core State Standards progress in difficulty through the grades, as is almost universal in curriculum documents. Sometimes it is helpful to "walk through" each standard, addressing a common text in order to clarify thinking about the escalating difficulty of the skills required by the standards.

Reading Anchor Standard 8: Delineate and evaluate the argument and specific claims in a text, including the validity of the reasoning as well as the relevance and sufficiency of the evidence.

Sample Argument

The school should provide pizza as an alternative for lunch one day each week. One way this would help the school is that the cafeteria would profit because more students would buy lunch on that day. To show how much money this might bring in, Mrs. Murphy's sixth-grade class took a survey of students in grades four through six, and 89 percent of the 182 students surveyed said they would buy pizza every week if they had an opportunity. For example, right now, on an average day, only 48 percent of the students buy lunch and the rest bring food from home.

Another important point is that students would throw away less food. If you watch students as they empty their trays in the lunchroom, the garbage they leave behind consists of many uneaten food items. However, on the days we have pizza, only a small part of the crust usually goes into the garbage.

[Added section for grade 8] In fact, if the cafeteria offered the students' least favorite lunch item (bean-broccoli casserole) every day, the waste would be far greater.

In conclusion, the school really needs to consider offering pizza for lunch at least once each week for the reasons listed, but also because students would be happier.

<u>CCSS.ELA-Literacy.RI.4.8:</u> Explain how an author uses reasons and evidence to support particular points in a text.

Grade 4: Explain how a writer supports points.

The writer uses the evidence in the survey and the information about watching students leave the lunchroom to support the points (claims) that more students would eat lunch and that students would throw away less uneaten food.

<u>CCSS.ELA-Literacy.RI.5.8:</u> Explain how an author uses reasons and evidence to support particular points in a text, **identifying which reasons and evidence support which point(s).**

Grade 5: Identify support for points.

- *The writer uses the survey data to support the point "...the cafeteria would profit because more students would buy lunch on that day."*
- *The point that "...students would throw away less food" is supported by the information about watching students leave the lunchroom, comparing the average day to a day on which they have pizza as an alternative lunch.*

<u>CCSS.ELA-Literacy.RI.6.8:</u> **Trace and evaluate the argument and specific claims** in a text, **distinguishing claims that are supported by reasons and evidence from claims that are not.**
Grade 6: Trace argument and claims.

- *The writer uses the survey data to support the reason "...the cafeteria would profit because more students would buy lunch on that day."*
- *The point that "...students would throw away less food" is supported by the information about watching students leave the lunchroom, comparing the average day to a day on which they have pizza as an alternative lunch.*
- *The writer offers no reasons or evidence to support the claim that students would be happier.*

Grade 6: Evaluate argument and claims. Distinguish supported claims/arguments from unsupported ones.

- *The claim that is supported by the survey is the strongest of the three claims, as it offers solid support from the survey. One possible way it might be weak is that some students might say now that they would buy pizza in order to influence the decision, but they might not actually buy it once per week if their parents decide that's too often to eat pizza or that it's too much money to spend every week.*
- *The information about watching students leave the lunchroom is actually quite weak. The writer does not tell us what "many uneaten food items" means. Just how many? How many of the trays have uneaten items? How much of each item is left? The reader does not know the answers to any of these questions, so that reason does not have strong support.*
- *The claim that students would be happier is just a value judgment by the writer, with no evidence to back it up, so it is the weakest argument of the three.*

<u>CCSS.ELA-Literacy.RI.7.8:</u> Trace and evaluate the argument and specific claims in a text, **assessing whether the reasoning is sound and the evidence is relevant and sufficient to support the claims.**
Grade 7: Assess reasoning and evidence. *(The other skills remain in place, with the addition of assessing.)*

Trace:

- *The writer uses the survey data to support the reason "...the cafeteria would profit because more students would buy lunch on that day." The point that "...students would throw away less food" is supported by the information about watching students leave the lunchroom, comparing the average day to a day on which they have pizza as an alternative lunch. The writer offers no reasons or evidence to support the claim that students would be happier.*

Evaluate:

- *The claim that is supported by the survey is the strongest of the three claims, as it offers solid support from the survey. One possible way it might be weak is that some students might say now that they would buy pizza in order to influence the decision, but they might not actually buy it once per week if their parents decide that's too often to eat pizza or that it's too much money to spend every week. The information about watching students leave the lunchroom is actually quite weak. The writer does not tell us what "many uneaten food items" means. Just how many? How many of the trays have uneaten items? How much of each item is left? The reader does not know the answers to any of these questions, so that reason does not have strong support.*

The claim that students would be happier is just a value judgment by the writer, with no evidence to back it up, so it is the weakest argument of the three.

Assess soundness and sufficiency:

- *Since two of the three points of support have weaknesses, overall this argument could use stronger evidence to support the claims.*
- *However, the data and reasons are all relevant because they all apply to the claim.*
- *Most schools would want to have a lunch program that profits, less food thrown away by students, and students who are basically happy every day.*

CCSS.ELA-Literacy.RI.8.8: **Delineate and evaluate** the argument and specific claims in a text, assessing whether the reasoning is sound and the evidence is relevant and sufficient; **recognize when irrelevant evidence is introduced.**

Grade 8: Delineate and evaluate.

- *The writer begins with the claim that "the school should provide pizza as an alternative for lunch one day each week." To a student, this may seem to be a strong argument, but adults might not agree, so the writer will need strong data and logical reasoning to support the claim.*
- *The writer uses survey data to support the reason "...the cafeteria would profit because more students would buy lunch on that day." This support is the strongest of the three in the argument because it provides survey data, but that data could be in question because it relies on students' answers, and parents often have strong control over student lunch choices. The survey would be stronger if parents had been included in the survey.*
- *The point that "...students would throw away less food" is supported by the information about watching students leave the lunchroom, comparing the average day to a day on which they have pizza as an alternative lunch. However, this is weak support because the decisions about how much food goes into the garbage is not explained. Just how much food ends up in the waste can? How many of the trays have uneaten items? How much of each item is left? The reader does not know the answers to any of these questions, so that reason does not have strong support. The question of how much food is wasted is a judgment by the writer, and we have no way of knowing if it is accurate.*
- *The writer could have interviewed lunchroom workers or the custodian to ask their opinions. They see the waste every day and would know more—and might offer opinions that carry more weight with the reader. We also don't know how long the observer watched, the number of days he/she watched, or the number of students that went past him/her.*
- *The writer offers no reasons or evidence to support the claim that students would be happier, so this is the weakest claim. Although most adults want students to be happier, happiness alone is not a reason to change a lunch program. Sometimes adults make decisions that they know won't make children happy. This is not entirely irrelevant, as adults do care about children's happiness, but it is not a strong argument.*

Recognize irrelevant evidence.

- *The claim that the savings would be even greater than it would be if the cafeteria offered bean-broccoli casserole every day is irrelevant. Increasing a statistical gap by creating a false situation is dishonest. Cafeteria supervisory personnel are well aware of foods students dislike.*

Appendix 6a: Blank Levels of Meaning Chart

Claims/Facts/Argument/Evidence	Topics	Concepts	Generalization/Principle	Theories

